Business Applications of Neural Networks

The State-of-the-Art of Real-World Applications

PROGRESS IN NEURAL PROCESSING

Series Advisors

Alan Murray *(University of Edinburgh)*
Lionel Tarassenko *(University of Oxford)*
Andreas S. Weigend *(Leonard N. Stern School of Business, New York University)*

Business Applications of Neural Networks

The State-of-the-Art of
Real-World Applications

Editors

Paulo J. G. Lisboa
Liverpool John Moores University, England

Bill Edisbury
Npower Ltd., England

Alfredo Vellido
Liverpool John Moores University, England

World Scientific
Singapore • New Jersey • London • Hong Kong

Published by

World Scientific Publishing Co. Pte. Ltd.

P O Box 128, Farrer Road, Singapore 912805

USA office: Suite 1B, 1060 Main Street, River Edge, NJ 07661

UK office: 57 Shelton Street, Covent Garden, London WC2H 9HE

British Library Cataloguing-in-Publication Data
A catalogue record for this book is available from the British Library.

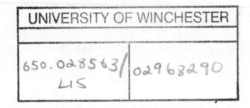
BUSINESS APPLICATIONS OF NEURAL NETWORKS: THE STATE-OF-THE-ART OF REAL WORLD APPLICATIONS

ISBN 981-02-4089-9

Printed in Singapore by World Scientific Printers

To Marisa and Txomin:

my parents, brave people.

Alfredo Vellido

Preface

Business Applications of Neural Networks

P.J.G. Lisboa and A. Vellido

School of Computing and Mathematical Sciences
Liverpool John Moores University
Liverpool L3 3AF, UK
E-mail: p.j.lisboa@livjm.ac.uk
http://www.cms.livjm.ac.uk/research/snc/neural.htm

1   Introduction

Business software is among the first commercially successful neural network products[1]. In a related real-world application, Air Canada uses neural networks for airport scheduling, reducing delays from flight re-scheduling, cutting fuel and other direct costs, and shortening the idle time of aircraft. This is typical of the effect of planning accuracy on the business operations, by allowing a rationalisation of the business process, affording greater speed and flexibility of response to customer demand, and potentially reducing the standing stock. In the particular application described by Bell *et alia*[1], a prediction is made of *no-shows*, an area where quantitative predictions are particularly difficult to model - *no-shows* are passengers who, for whatever reason, do not board, thus enabling airlines to overbook their flights, hedging the risk of overestimating the *no-shows*, against lost revenue by underestimating them. It is an example of a resource allocation problem in an environment that is unstable. In an unrelated application, at Kodak, the use of neural networks for optimal resource allocation is claimed to have reduced production costs by $3 million per year. Changing business again, to the electricity industry, these new methods have become the yardstick for demand forecasting. All of these processes share a substantial degree of complexity in the process to be modelled, for which there is little information available about effective model structures.

The particular approach used for scheduling relies on the availability of time-delayed feedback about the accuracy of the predicted *no-shows*, and requires a highly specialised model. However, standard neural networks have found a large number of more routine applications in quantitative business analysis, from fraud risk prediction, through credit scoring, to customer profiling. Each of these application areas is represented in the case studies selected for this book.

In fraud detection, for instance, two software packages have become the industry standard - Falcon and PRISM. They are based on neural networks, and are designed to interface with the current business software for credit card management. Both hold impressive corporate accounts, and command substantial fees. The business case to offset their costs is based on their expected performance, but their accuracy at detection fraudulent credit requests for different credit card products depends very substantially on the particular design of the neural network.

Moreover, data analysis is increasingly important for corporate decision making. All of the major statistical houses are developing specialist tools for predictive modelling, automatic segmentation, and visualisation of complex databases, with the goal of turning the large volumes of data generated by the business process into useful knowledge for the business managers.

How do neural networks relate to statistical methods? What do they offer that is new in data processing and, how does this contribute added value to the business? How do neural networks work, in practice?

2   What are neural networks?

There is a consensus emerging that we are moving from an industrial society to a knowledge-based society, no longer dominated by labour and raw materials costs, but driven by information, much of it now captured at the point of sale, or generated directly from the transaction with the client. This is a trend which electronic data interchange and electronic commerce accelerate still further. Any company's most valuable asset, at the core of competitive advantage, is its knowledge about the business, which is present in two quite distinct forms. The first is explicit business understanding, and the second is implicit in the electronic and other databases. This section is about neural networks as tools to derive useful information directly from the data. This usually takes place using a combination of two complementary processes - segmentation of the data into meaningful clusters contained similar data types, and predictive modelling as required, for instance, in demand forecasting.

Artificial neural networks is a term used to describe a gross analogy with the processing of information in biological nervous systems. They are characterised by arrays of highly interconnected cells, often arranged in layered structures, where each cell, or neuron, is roughly similar to the next. It has long been known that learning involves changes to the links between neural cells, the synaptic connections[2], so that stored memories are contained in the links between neuronal cells, rather than in the cells themselves. The role of the neuron is to weight-up the total input received through the links with other cells, the result of which will be to stimulate, or inhibit, its firing rate. The variable synaptic strengths and the straightforward response of the neuron, are captured in a simple model shown in figure 1. The saturation curve in figure 2 represents the neuron's firing rate, which reduces under inhibition, or negative activation, and increases under positive excitation up to a maximum firing frequency, denoted here as a unity response.

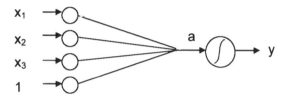

Figure 1: Model of an artificial neural cell. The essential features of neural networks are the interconnection between cells through synapses whose strength is carefully adjusted to store data patterns, together with a characteristic response curve limited from above and below by complete cell inactivity, and saturation. In this figure, *a*, represents the sum total of the activation received by the cell, who responds with a firing rate, *y*. Note the constant input of unity, which biases the cell's response.

This arrangement of replica cells into neural networks is known to have powerful pattern recognition properties, in particular the capability to smoothly associate the response to new stimuli, or input data, with the correct response observed for previously experienced stimuli, or historical data. To see this, consider a small example of four historical data points, representing a hypothetical credit risk scenario where young age and low income results in low risk, either attribute rising on its own becomes a high risk, but old age with large investment income returns to low risk. This is an example of a non-linear function, since the trend in risk rising which each attribute, is then negated when both attributes are simultaneously high. The logic of this function, the eXclusive-OR (XOR), is summarized in Table 1.

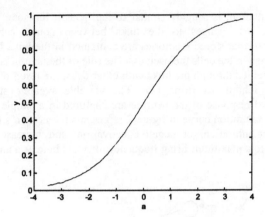

Figure 2: Typical response function for a single neuron. This curve has the functional form $y = 1/[1+\exp(-a)]$.

The illustrative data for this simplified credit risk example, for the input into a single linear cell, are shown in figure 3. The first input to the cell, x_1, is a continuous code for age, the next code, x_2, represents total household income, and y is credit risk. An interaction between the two attributes is expressed by a third input which is high when only one of the two variables is high, $x_3 = 1 - x_1.x_2$. Finally, we shall assume also a gating input whose activity is purely inhibitory, i.e. -1, which in a biological analogy, serves as gating input, setting a minimum stimulus threshold to elicit a response from the cell.

input x1	input x2	cell response y
0	0	0
0	1	1
1	0	1
1	1	0

Table 1: XOR logical function in the illustrative example in the text.

This simple cell is described by four parameters, each setting a synaptic strength, or network weights. These weights can now be configured to store the observed data patterns, for instance requiring the cell to selectively respond to the combinations of $(x_1, x_2, response)$ in table 1.

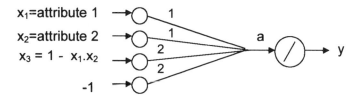

x₁=attribute 1
x₂=attribute 2
x₃ = 1 - x₁.x₂

Figure 3: Example of a single neural cell, in this example exhibiting a linear response to the network activation. If the synaptic strengths assume the values shown, this cell will correctly recall four data patterns which represent previously observed data.

Setting the network weights as shown in figure 3 recalls the required data patterns, as can readily be verified by direct calculation of the cell's response, which is $y = x1+x2+2*(1-x1.x2)-2 = x1+x2-2*x1.x2$. Moreover, the cell will respond to a continuous range of inputs, beyond the binary values originally provided as training data to set the network weights. This is illustrated graphically in figure 4.

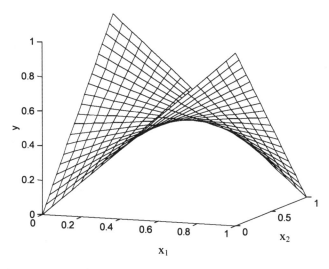

Figure 4: Response surface of the cell model described in figure 3. Notice that the data used to configure the cell weights, represented by circles, is correctly recalled, since the surface passes through each of the four points. However, the cell also responds to intermediate input values. Contour maps of the response are also shown.

In summary, besides storing four input-response combinations using four weight-strengths, the capacity of the cell to smoothly interpolate the response for intermediate data is this cell's implementation of the associative memory function.

If any of the weight parameters were modified, this would alter the response surface and thus corrupt all of the stored memories, that is to say the response at the corners of the plot. It follows that each stored memory is partly contained in every network weight, which is known as distributed storage of information, and is another key feature in biological neural networks. It can also be seen that the half-height contours of the response surface define a partition of the input space into sectors. This can be used as a classification tool, to assign regions of data into labelled sectors, e.g. 'good' and 'bad' creditors might correspond to regions of high and low cell responses, respectively. This gives the model predictive power to quantify the expected risk for future applicants, based on the storage of historical data from creditors followed through to complete payment, or default, in previously approved loans.

The computational model for data storage using software emulations of artificial neural networks must now be given a statistical perspective. This is because, in the real world, customer data from different classes of applicant do not usually separate neatly into distinct clusters. Rather, they have a tendency to mix, so that decisions near the boundary between different customer categories have to be made on the balance of probabilities.

It can be shown[3] that, in the characteristic sigmoid response curve shown previously in figure 2, the value of the cell's output, y, accurately represents the conditional probability of class membership, when the two classes to be separated are normally distributed with a common covariance matrix. The argument of the network output, $a=log(y/(1-y))$, is nothing more than the logarithm of the odds in favour of one particular class assignment, for which the probability of class membership is y. This simple credit risk example is analogous to the standard statistical procedure employed for credit scoring, where each attribute is assigned an independent coefficient, or score, and interacting variables are explicitly modelled, usually through additional polynomial terms.

Neural networks are particularly useful when the form of interactions in the data is unknown, where it is advantageous to directly model non-linearities in the multivariate sense, rather than to split fields separately into categorical attribute vectors, and when distributional assumptions are to be avoided. In this case, the model must approximate with arbitrary accuracy general non-linear functions of multiple variables, requiring an extension of the predictive model from containing a single cell, into a neural network with two, or more, layers of adjustable weights[3], shown in figure 5.

The cell layer sandwiched between the input nodes on the left, and the response nodes on the right, in figure 5, is called a hidden layer. The network weights are estimated using variants of gradient descent algorithms, taking into account the complexity of the network, through the inclusion, in the objective function, of penalty terms to suppress unnecessary weights. These procedures are detailed by Bishop[3], along with their essential role in allowing the network to fit arbitrary non-linear functions well matched to the structure of the data, while preventing the network from fitting the noise that is inevitably present in the data, a well known pitfall of non-linear models that is called over-fitting.

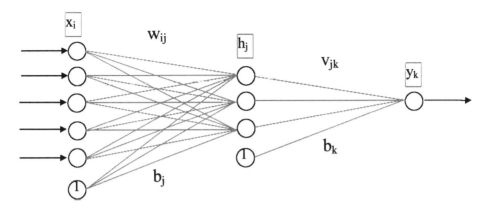

Figure 5: A Multi-layer Perceptron (MLP) neural network. The network inputs are labelled *x*, the hidden nodes by *h* and the predicted output by *y*. The remaining symbols indicate connection weights, *w* and *v*, and threshold values, *b*.

There are alternative predictive neural network models, for instance using cells with localised responses to adapt the shape of the response surface preferentially to data in limited regions in the input space. Examples of this approach are the Radial Basis Function network and the Restricted Coulomb Energy network, featuring in a later chapter of this book.

Turning our attention to data segmentation, the role of the neural network now becomes to model recurrent patterns in the data, in order to identify typical data segments which may be labelled, and may merit separate analysis resulting in predictive causal or statistical models tailored separately for each segment. Several chapters of the book deal with unsupervised neural networks for segmentation, illustrating in detail the role of this type of models for the visualisation of high-dimensional data using two and three-dimensional maps. These maps reflect the topology of the data, that is to say, the neighbourhood relationships between the data points are mapped to into the nearby projections of those points onto the neural network. This can be accomplished without any need for prior class labelling. The best known of these segmentation models is the Self-Organising Map (SOM).

Just as the MLP is the neural network extension of logistic regression into a flexible non-linear discriminant model, so the SOM extends classical clustering algorithms, such as k-means clustering, into topologically organised data projection maps with significantly enhanced power for data visualisation.

Furthermore, both the MLP and SOM can be formulated within a rigorous statistical framework, which provides confident predictions with robustness against over-fitting the data. These models are known as the Bayesian neural network and the GTM, and they are further described in the chapter on eCommerce.

Finally, before leaving this introductory section, it is worth pointing out the potential advantages of exploratory data analysis using unsupervised models, even where predictive models are sought. This arises because data patterns – representing, for instance, retail customers, credit applicants, or even companies in danger of financial distress - that are assigned similar risk scores, may consist of an eclectic mix of quite different segments, all incurring similar risks, but for quite different reasons. In this case, a supplementary visualisation of the data permits a more accurate interpretation of the results from the predictive model, sometimes permitting even an explanation of the predictions made. This is how the business expertise integrates with the data-based training and evaluation of statistical or neural network models, and forms a key component in understanding the models obtained, in order to make the results useful for the company.

3 Putting neural networks to work

A recent survey by the authors[4], comprising published research in the period 1992-1998 gives an overview of the extensive range of neural network applications in business. The main neural network application areas can be roughly summarised as Accounting and Auditing, Finance (with the main body of research focusing on bankruptcy prediction and credit evaluation), Management/Decision Making and Marketing. This survey revealed that most of the research (over an 85% of the studies) used supervised models, mainly the MLP trained with back-propagation.

It is interesting to discover which are the main contributions of the neural network models to the business application at hand, according to the authors reviewed in the survey. These are summarised in table 2, from the most to the less frequently quoted, starting from the top row.

CONTRIBUTIONS OF THE NNs TO THE BUSINESS APPLICATION
1. Neural Networks outperform other models in the business application.
2. Neural Networks yield similar results to other models in the business application.
3. Neural Networks perform worse than other models in the business application.
4. One type of Neural Networks outperforms others.
5. Hybridazing Neural Networks with other models provides improved results.
6. Neural Networks show promise for future developments of the business application.
7. Neural Networks offer new insights into the business application.
8. Neural Networks meet the challenge of a "real-world" business application.

Table 2: Main contributions of neural networks to the studies reviewed in Vellido *et alia*[4], ranked in the order of the frequency with which these conclusions arise in published work.

This review also compares the most frequently adduced advantages and disadvantages of neural network methodologies in their research context. They are summarised in table 3, once again in order and with the most frequent in the top row.

Some of the frequently made comments summarised in table 3 are actively being addressed by the research community. The purpose of this book is to illustrate practical applications through real-world case studies, and also to indicate best practice in neural network design. In particular, the objections raised in table 3 with regard to systematic network design, robust generalisation and transparency, all reflect key characteristics required of practical commercial systems. These issues have been addressed in the following chapters, though in different ways.

The design of business systems must begin with a careful selection of attributes, which, for instance, in the case of credit card fraud corresponds to a carefully crafted customer profile. With neural networks, data representation is how business expertise is introduced into the model. Now we come to robustness in the generalisation of model predictions for new data. A successful transition from the computer laboratory to the marketplace relies on painstaking performance evaluation. This will rely on having enough representative data to enable the network designer to estimate the network weights from training data, setting the training parameters to optimise its performance for validation data, while keeping a 'hold-out' sample for a final performance evaluation.

ADVANTAGES of NEURAL NETS	DISADVANTAGES of NEURAL NETS
High accuracy: NNs are able to approximate complex non-linear mappings.	Poor transparency: NNs operate as "black boxes".
Independence from prior assumptions: NNs do not make *a priori* assumptions about the distribution of the data, or the form of interactions between factors.	Trial-and-error design: the selection of the hidden nodes and training parameters is heuristic.
Noise tolerance: NNs are very flexible with respect to incomplete, missing and noisy data.	Data hungry: estimating the network weights requires large amounts of data, and this can be very computer intensive.
Ease of maintenance: NN models can be updated with fresh data, making them useful for dynamic environments.	Over-fitting: if too many weights are used without regularisation makes, NNs become useless in terms of generalisation to new data.
NNs overcome some limitations of other statistical methods, while generalizing them.	There is no explicit set of rules to select the most suitable NN algorithm.
Hidden nodes, in supervised NN models can be regarded as latent variables.	NNs are totally dependent on the quality and amount of data available.
NNs can be implemented in parallel hardware.	NNs may converge to local minima in the error surface.
Neural Networks performance can be highly automated, minimizing human involvement.	NN techniques are still rapidly evolving and they are not yet robust.
NNs are especially suited to tackle problems in non-conservative domains.	NNs lack classical statistical properties. Confidence intervals and hypothesis testing are not available.

Table 3: Main advantages and disadvantages of the application of neural network models, according to the surveyed studies[4].

Moreover, well established statistical frameworks which can be used to condition the network design, ensuring that the uncertainties contained in the neural network model, are themselves used to moderate the network predictions towards a safe guessing-line[3]. The application of statistical principles in neural network design is as relevant to unsupervised models, for market segmentation, as it is to predictive models. These are practical methodologies which are the recommended route to get the maximum amount of useful information out of the data, removing the vagaries of trial-and-error design, and controlling the risk of overfitting. In regression, the use of regularised cost functions gives stable confidence intervals around the network predictions.

Diverse neural network models have been described and utilized throughout this book. For convenience, they are summarized in figure 6, including pointers to the chapters in which they have been applied.

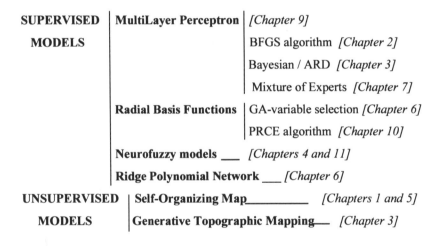

SUPERVISED | **MultiLayer Perceptron** | *[Chapter 9]*
MODELS | | BFGS algorithm *[Chapter 2]*
| | Bayesian / ARD *[Chapter 3]*
| | Mixture of Experts *[Chapter 7]*
| **Radial Basis Functions** | GA-variable selection *[Chapter 6]*
| | PRCE algorithm *[Chapter 10]*
| **Neurofuzzy models** ___ *[Chapters 4 and 11]*
| **Ridge Polynomial Network** ___ *[Chapter 6]*
UNSUPERVISED | **Self-Organizing Map**_____ *[Chapters 1 and 5]*
MODELS | **Generative Topographic Mapping**___ *[Chapter 3]*

Figure 6: Summary of the diverse neural network models used in this book.

4   Overview of the book

This book contains illustrative case studies from real-world business applications of neural networks. Each chapter describes the business application, detailing the role of predictive and exploratory models for that application area. In order to focus the contents of the book, applications were selected from three areas of particular business interest, and where the use of neural network methods is well developed. They are marketing/forecasting, fraud detection and risk assessment.

Between them, the case studies cover the most widely used neural computing paradigms, including advanced developments of this technology which are close to the state-of-the-art. In addition, in the area of fraud detection, where neural network products have been commercially very successful, two leading product suppliers have been invited to provide some insight into the neural network component of their software.

In all case studies, the added-value from using neural networks is pointed out, together with more technical aspects of their practical implementation, application to the business environment -including the issues involved in building appropriate data representations that are effective for the business application- and, finally, the requirement to integrate with current business systems and the impact on operational protocols, where appropriate.

This book follows-on from earlier publications on the application of neural networks to finance. Many of these deal specifically with securities trading and other esoteric aspects of investment management, but there are those which include a substantial focus on areas of interest to retail, banking and insurance, e.g. Goonatilake and Treleaven[5]. There are also more general accounts of intelligent systems applications in knowledge discovery generally, although these tend to be very qualitative[6]. Our compilation of case-studies attempts to provide a balance between offering a perspective of the benefits of this technology to the business, and the practical aspects of implementing pilot studies, through to fully commercial products.

The first three chapters of the book concern marketing problems and, more specifically, market segmentation.

In **Chapter 1**, travel preference data from British Airways are analysed using the SOM, with the aim of improving the business-customer relationship. **Chapter 2** deals with the extraction of rules from neural networks in order to characterise IT adoption by private companies. The business-to-consumer electronic commerce market is explored and segmented in **Chapter 3**, using statistically sound supervised and unsupervised networks.

Then, the next three chapters explore, from new perspectives, two classic finance problems: bankruptcy prediction and credit scoring.

Chapter 4 hybridises the concepts of fuzzy logic and supervised neural networks into a neuro-fuzzy model for bankruptcy prediction, whereas **Chapter 5** lies down the guidelines for best practices in the application of the SOM to the same problem. **Chapter 6** provides a very practical insight into the nature and development of scorecards for Equifax, and the role played by neural networks for credit scoring.

Fraud detection, one of the applications for which neural networks have been most successful in terms of commercial deployment, is the subject of the following four chapters.

The general strategies for exploiting neural networks in retail finance, including a credit card fraud detection case study, are introduced in **Chapter 7**. This is followed by **Chapter 8**, which gives account of a joint project, involving Vodafone, Siemens and Logica UK, to tackle fraud in mobile communications. It includes an in-depth analysis of the legal issues conditioning this subject. In **Chapter 9**, the use of the neural network-based Falcon™ product from HNC software, for payment card fraud detection, is illustrated. **Chapter 10** analyses another commercial product: PRISM™, from Nestor, based on Radial Basis Function networks, for money laundering detection.

Finally, **Chapter 11** provides a general overview of the application of neuro-fuzzy models in different business areas.

References

1. T.M. Bell, W.R. Hutchinson and K.R. Stephens. 1992. Using adaptive networks for resource allocation in changing environments. In *Neural networks-current applications*, P.J.G. Lisboa, ed. (London: Chapman and Hall).

2. W.S. McCullough and W. Pitts. 1943. A logical calculus of the ideas immanent in nervous activity. *Bull. Math. Biophys.*, **5**, 115-133.

3. C.M. Bishop 1995 *Neural networks for pattern recognition*. Oxford University Press.

4. A. Vellido, P.J.G. Lisboa and J. Vaughan. 1999. Neural networks in business: a survey of applications (1992-1998). *Expert Systems with Applications,* **17**(1), 51-70.

5. S. Goonatilake and P. Treleaven (eds.) 1995. *Intelligent systems for finance and business* (New York: John Wiley).

6. V. Dhar and R. Stein. 1997. Seven methods for transforming corporate data into business intelligence (Prentice Hall: New Jersey).

Contents

Chapter 1

On the Use of Neural Networks for Analysing Travel Preference Data

Simon Cummings
British Airways Plc.

1   Introduction: Description of the business area

British Airways as an international airline has as its mission "to be the undisputed leader in world travel". It is a company which has hitherto concentrated its efforts on the high-revenue, business travel end of the market. British Airways, in common with many other airlines, has for a considerable time had a frequent flyer loyalty scheme, which British Airways calls the Executive Club, aimed in particular at those who travel frequently as part of their work. This programme rewards frequent travellers with "miles" which can be redeemed for free flights and "points" which count towards higher levels or tiers of membership which confer access to lounges and other convenience benefits. To complement this, as a way of serving the leisure market, in 1997 British Airways launched a separate concept known as the Travel Service, which sets out to provide an added-value service for leisure travellers.

The Travel Service, with a membership in the UK, is primarily a scheme whereby preference information given by members on their enrolment forms is used to guide selection and matching of suitable special offers. The offers mainly consist of holidays and flights but may also include activities within the home country such as theme parks and theatrical events.

In this paper the example of the Travel Service will be used to illustrate some points relating to the use of data mining and neural networks to analyse customer data. Increasingly in today's world companies are routinely collecting data on their customers and transactions. The terms "relationship marketing" and "customer relationship management" have come to symbolise companies' desire to use customer data to gain an increased understanding of customer requirements. More than that, companies are seeking to create, on a large and often automated scale, the "relationship" which customers might feel dealing with a local shop where they are well known and the retailer anticipates their wishes and expectations. On the other hand, the use of data by large, possibly impersonal-seeming corporate organisations, to fuel an ever-increasing industry of direct mail, is often perceived as junk mail, and regarded as unwelcome and inappropriate. In the near future we shall increasingly see the use of multiple electronic media as a vehicle for this kind of marketing communication. It is therefore important that the "blanket" or indiscriminate use of direct mail is kept under control, and that an effort is made to improve the appropriateness of the message to the customer's situation and needs. To this end, the goal of database segmentation and customer profiling is to identify kinds of customers with differing needs and to provide appropriate offers and loyalty incentives, as well as identifying customers who are likely responders or good prospects. These ideas are particularly well developed in the retail and financial services industries.

It is now well known that artificial neural network methods can provide a way of seeking patterns and clusters in data and of using those patterns to estimate probabilities of a certain outcome or the propensity towards a certain action or behaviour, based on past data. For an introduction to different methods for data mining, or knowledge discovery from databases, see for example Adriaans & Zantinge[1], and for practical guidelines on the application of neural networks, see also Tarassenko[2].

Neural networks fall into two distinct categories, supervised and unsupervised learning. Typically an unsupervised learning method will be used for the pattern or cluster discovery and indeed such methods have very strong similarities to cluster analysis techniques in the traditional statistical literature. For propensity modelling and probability estimation, a feed-forward neural network method such as the multi-layer perceptron[3], or radial basis function networks[4,5] would be used. These methods extend naturally from the techniques of linear and logistic regression. These neural network architectures form a method of estimating posterior probabilities, which is non-linear in the parameters of the model. This means that neural networks of these types should be good at characterising "local" behaviour where the interactions of a number of variables are important. For a thorough treatment of the use of feed-forward neural networks, and in particular of issues relating to regarding their outputs as probabilities, see, for example, Bishop[6]. Further information on the relationship of neural networks to other statistical methods can be found in Ripley[7].

A neural net can be used to analyse any data that can be tabulated in such a form that a number of inputs or independent variables map on to, or influence, one or more outputs (dependent variables). A network is typically "trained" on a sample of historic data. This means that a training algorithm essentially an iterative optimisation scheme adapts the values of the model's internal parameters or weights, until a convergent solution is reached which has a minimum value, or at least a local minimum, of the error or difference between the model's estimate of the output variable and the true value of the output variable. A second set of data is used to ensure that the structural parameters of the network (for example, the number of hidden units and the number of iterations used) are such that the network produces a model which will generalise well to hitherto unseen data, rather than "overfitting" by representing in detail the random peculiarities of the sample of data used for training. The network's performance is then measured in terms of a third set of data as the first two have both been "seen" or used to influence the model.

In the case of an unsupervised or self-organising network, such as Kohonen's Self-organising Feature Map[8,9] (SOM), the network consists of a "competitive" layer, where the node with the "best" value is considered the "winner". Usually for a given numeric input record, the value concerned is the generalised "distance" between the input record and the weight values linking the input layer to the relevant node in the competitive layer. The Euclidean distance is usually used. The weights to the winning node and others in its neighbourhood are adjusted to lie closer to the values of the input record, and the process is repeated many times, going through the training records at random, gradually reducing the size of the neighbourhood surrounding the winning node, within which the adjustments are made. The net result of this process, when it has converged, is that data points which are close together in the original data are represented by points close together in the "Kohonen" layer (usually a square or oblong 2-dimensional grid of units). Each node in the 2-dimensional grid layer has weights from all the inputs. If the inputs are normalised (*i.e.* scaled so that they lie between 0 and 1, or -1 and 1) and the weights are on the same scale, then the set of weights from the input to the 2-d grid is a vector which describes a typical value in the data, effectively a cluster centre. The cluster related to it is defined by the set of data points for which that node is the one with the smallest distance. Thus the grid shows, clearly in two dimensions, clusters of data points. In the original data these are in a high number of dimensions (*i.e.* characterised by the values of a large number of variables) and may be difficult to visualise.

Nevertheless, one can cover much of the ground required in profiling and segmentation using conventional querying languages and exploratory statistics. Data visualisation techniques in commercial statistical packages are becoming increasingly sophisticated. So why, in this application, is there a need for a new technical solution? The use of the self-organising map gives a powerful visualisation tool for observing the typical values of different variables for the different clusters. This can be done by examination of the weight matrix or by visually overlaying a set of diagrams, which show the effect of different individual variables, and looking at the combined effect of many inputs. It assists in identifying the level of complexity (the intrinsic dimensionality) in the problem, as expressed in the data, and allows for a rapid appraisal of the number of clusters. Outliers in multidimensional data can be identified by examining the minimum of the distances between the data records and the prototype or cluster centre vectors and looking for high values.

In a marketing application, where the input data may be buying patterns or customer preference data, the prototypes show combinations of attributes that illustrate traits in buying behaviour for different groups of customers. Furthermore, because adjoining grid nodes represent groups that are in conceptually close together in the original data, it can allow for cross-selling or the introduction to customers of new ideas in a controlled and rational way.

Another advantage of this method is that by varying the size of the grid, one can vary the extent of detail that is picked out. It is often very useful to have an overview, broad-brush model to show the principal effects in the data. This can be used to direct the application of data mining effort to the most promising sectors of the customer base.

2   Design

The idea behind this aspect of the travel service is that the preference information supplied (and updated at suitable intervals) is used to provide "matched" offers from British Airways, its holiday subsidiary British Airways Holidays or from a selected third party company. Due to systems and practical limitations of performing a full-scale individualised matching and personalised mailing, a data mining approach had been taken.

The approach taken in this work was to use self-organising maps to segment the preference data set at a number of different levels of detail, and to use 'if..then' rules to define subsets of the database for the purpose of sending targeted mailings.

On their application forms, members had been asked to provide details of their holiday preferences and travel patterns, such as which destinations they had recently visited and planned to visit in the next eighteen months, and in which parts of the world they had visited friends and relatives. Preferred activities on holiday were also noted, such as skiing, golf, other sports, cultural tours, fine dining, opera and theatre, *etc.*, as were customers' preferences for types of holidays, *i.e.* packages *versus* flight only, flight plus villa, fly-drive, *etc.* Some demographic information was gathered: address, age and sex, also amount spent on leisure travel per year and typical number of holidays and short breaks taken, and whether the applicant was also a member of a frequent flyer or mileage collection scheme.

The data consisted of around 260,000 records, with over 150 fields. For the purposes of the data mining tasks, the number of fields selected was reduced to sixty. The implementation of self-organising maps used was that in the NeuralWorks software[10]. In the first instance, a sample of about 12000 records was taken and a 4 by 4 grid was used, generating 16 "cells" or clusters. Analysing the weights from each of the inputs to each of the 16 cluster nodes gave a profile or prototypical behaviour for each cluster. It was also possible to see how close the clusters were, conceptually, to one another. It was found that for the purposes required, many of the clusters were similar and could be grouped together. Hence six to seven groups were identified, which was seen as a suitable number for a trial of the approach. Some of the clusters were easily characterised into prototypical customer types; others were more diverse and contained more structure. With these clusters, a further analysis, or "micro-clustering" was performed, again using a self-organising map but with a larger number of nodes (100). In this case, although there are too many clusters to be useful in marketing terms, the technique provides a very effective visualisation of the overlapping groupings in the data. In particular, destination, time of year and activity combinations are easily visualised, together with patterns in expenditure, frequency of holidays, and demographics.

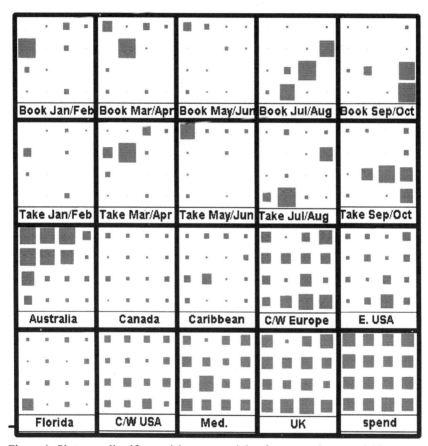

Figure 1: Sixteen-cell self-organising map weights for twenty input variables.

Figure 1 shows a typical display from the self-organising map analysis. Here we see the results of training a 4 by 4 SOM (giving sixteen prototypes or clusters). This number was chosen fairly arbitrarily, but subsequent analysis showed it to be suitable given the number of true groupings and the level of complexity which suited the business requirements. In the diagram, the weights from the input layer to the Kohonen layer are displayed in a sequence of Hinton diagrams, one for each of twenty input variables chosen from a total of sixty inputs. The variables shown represent preferred time of year for booking and taking a holiday, destination preferences and level of expenditure. The area of the square "blobs" is proportional to the magnitude of the weights in each case. It is important to note that the numbers of people in the clusters will not be uniform, though there is a parameter in the model that can be adjusted to vary the extent to which the cluster sizes differ.

In practice, for those variables with a possible state of 0 or 1, the size of the square blobs represent the proportion of respondents within each cluster who indicated that preference. By "overlaying" in ones mind the maps for the different variables, some patterns can be discerned, for example one can detect (within the validity of the preference data) which groups tend to book early or late, or when people who intend to travel to certain destinations wish to travel, *etc.*

There are some caveats here about taking these results too literally, and they centre around the fact that although one has distinct facts from the form data about various attributes, *e.g.* one might know that a certain individual has a preference for golf, for Australia and for booking in September, this does not imply that any combination of these is necessarily true. He or she may play golf in September but do something different when in Australia, and so on. Thus these diagrams and the numbers underlying them should be used only as a statistical guide indicating general propensities.

In terms of implementation, the output of the neural network was not used directly, at least initially, to produce the lists used for mailing, although this would be possible. Instead the data mining results were used in conjunction with domain knowledge, details of availability and experimental design and hypothesis testing considerations, to construct appropriate rules and queries for data extraction.

3   Impact of practical issues

Most examples of data analysis and data mining will be affected by missing or unreliable data values in some way. The way in which missing values are dealt with depends critically upon the nature of the data set itself, on the context and real-world meaning of the variables, and on the process by which the data were collected, *etc.* In some cases the absence of a value may itself be a useful piece of information. It is also important to avoid coding of missing values which distort the distribution of the data, for example, if a number is on a scale of 1 to 5, coding the missing values as 6. In early stages of the analysis, missing data was coded by defining additional indicator variables for fields which had large numbers of missing values and setting these to 1 if the corresponding variable value was missing.

Although the self-organising map is not so much affected by the problem of certain classes having uneven prior probabilities, there may be some effects due to low prior probabilities on some of the input variables. In the weight update equation $\delta w^r = \alpha \left(w^r - x^r \right)$, the weight vector w^r is updated by a vector amount δw^r which is given by a learning rate α multiplied by the vector difference between the weight vector and the input vector (the current record), the ith

component relating to the ith input variable. Variables with low prior probabilities will have a weak effect on the network's learning (*i.e.* there will rarely be a large component in the direction of x_i), so the resulting weights may be more dependent on the random initialisation of the network.

There are also some more subtle practical aspects of working with real-world data. One of these involves ensuring that the data are up to date. Apart from the basic questions of maintaining personal information such as addresses *etc.*, there is the question of what is the "shelf-life" of preference data. It can safely be assumed that activity preferences may change less frequently than destination preferences, for example, but such questions need to be addressed when considering using past data to support future decisions. Another subtlety resides in the "psychological" or human-factors aspects of form-filling. Effects, which we have identified in this project, are wishful thinking, misreading of the form, and the general subtle differences in understanding of commonly used terms between different people. Position of questions on the form may also be important. An example of "wishful thinking" was the "Australia effect", where a large percentage of respondents ticked the box asking "do you intend to visit Australasia in the next eighteen months?". This preference indication is not borne out by bookings and is out of scale with the preferences for more achievable destinations. While it may be true that many of the members do wish to travel round the world, it would also be the case that many are "dreaming"! An example of potential misreading or misunderstanding is where two separate questions on the form related to the month in which the customer *books* a holiday and the month in which they *take* a holiday. Analysis of the preference form data showed that many people claim to book and take in the same adjacent pair of months, while analysis of the booking data shows this mostly not to be the case. As a possible example of differences in understanding of a term, consider that one of the questions on the form was "how interested are you in last minute offers? (Not at all, slightly or very interested?)". When it comes to booking holidays, different people may have different ideas of what constitutes "last minute"! However, the purpose of this discussion is not to criticise the design of an application form, but rather to point out that even some straightforward-looking response data may generate points to watch for when carrying out the analysis, whether using a neural net or more conventional means. Furthermore, the data mining analysis can provide pointers for interpretation of form data and perhaps considerations for design improvements.

4   Advantages and limitations

Advantages of using the self-organising map for this kind of segmentation are mainly those of flexibility and a "soft" approach. The granularity of the segmentation can be chosen to fit with the complexity of the underlying problem, as manifested in the data.   Importantly also it can be chosen to match the level of complexity with which the business is comfortable, operationally and in terms of implementation and support. For example, in a customer data application one may be able, technically, to perform a segmentation into dozens of clusters but it may only be possible or economically feasible, to discriminate the service or product in a small number of ways. In such a case, what is gained by such an exercise is a deeper understanding of how the service or product relates to different groups of customers. However, at the end of the day the implemented model has to be simple enough to be understood, sense-checked and resourced. With the advent of electronic commerce and intelligent software agents, these limitations will begin to recede.

A data mining model of this type can be seen as aiding the generation of *hypotheses* to be tested, as well as proving or disproving hypotheses arising from business knowledge or judgement. Note that when we are using the terms "prove" and "disprove" here, their meaning is to be understood as limited within the scope and accuracy of the available data. Additionally, issues of experimental design and the selection of control groups become important here. In a business context there is often tension between the requirements of scientific rigour in order to draw firm conclusions, and the imperative of the business not to miss opportunities or turn away good custom.

For complete rigour it is necessary to test potential conclusions from a data mining model against the raw data, i.e. to check that the profiles and properties of clusters or segments as produced by the data mining model are indeed seen to be present when analysing the data variable by variable. Furthermore it is important to check that ones understanding of the real-world definition, meaning and quality of the data is correct. Here it is important to look at process issues where the data is collected. If the data is gathered from an application form for example, different people may attach different understandings to the same question. Different operators may have different styles and emphases when issuing forms to customers, *etc.* In this work it was found that there was a cluster of customers whose booking rate was about four times the average but for whom much of the data on the application form was missing. It turned out that these were members who were enrolled whilst in a travel shop during a campaign when there was an incentive (prize draw, for instance) for joining the Travel Service. It would appear that for this segment of passengers, due to operational time constraints only a minimal number of details had been entered for each person.

It is appropriate to look at some of the limitations of neural network methods as well as their advantages. A technical limitation of the approach is the fact that the SOM has a dependency on the (random) order in which the data is presented to it, and can exhibit artefacts due to "folds" in the topology of the way the data is mapped onto the grid. In view of this, it is always wise to check the cluster contents back against the original data, using queries and frequency plots to understand the extent to which the clusters are separate or overlap.

In business terms, a limitation of a "soft" cluster model, where the membership of a cluster can be described only in terms of the model itself, rather than by a simple rule or query, is that if the results are to be used for personal communication, one loses the impact of being able to give a reason or explanation as to why a particular communication has been chosen for a particular person. This limitation can be avoided by using rules to approximate the clusters derived by the self-organising map. Some accuracy is lost in order to gain clarity of message.

Any model, whether a classical statistical one or a neural network, is prone to changes in business process over time. For example, in this instance, during the period of running a controlled trial of the model, changes were made in the way in which bookings were routed and identified. These changes meant that the data that indicated which of the bookings received by British Airways and British Airways Holidays were attributable to the Travel Service, became unreliable.

It is of course possible to pursue clustering, profiling and segmentation applications using conventional methods. Typically this would be done either using cluster analysis, regression and correlation analysis, or by choosing variables of interest and performing a sequence of queries to understand the overlaps and correlations between different data variables. Cluster centres in a cluster analysis are analogous to the prototype vectors in a self-organising map. The advantages of the neural network method over cluster analysis lie firstly in the visualisation power of the self-organising map; secondly in its topology-preserving property, that is cells which are close physically in the 2-dimensional map relate to customer groups who are conceptually or behaviourally similar and thirdly in its flexibility, in that different levels of granularity can be observed by varying the number of cells in the Kohonen layer. It is also possible to control the extent to which the cluster sizes are similar. This is done in the SOM using a parameter known as the "conscience" parameter (supposedly because it prevents one node from winning too frequently).

In this application it is useful to know the populations of different "cells" within the data space, that is, the number of people in various categories defined by combinations of variables. For example, one may wish to know how many people are interested in skiing and golf, and then to find out, within the data, what other interests they have expressed, what destinations they prefer, what type of holiday package they are interested in (e.g. flight only or fly-drive or all-inclusive), and so on.

5   Practical difficulties with specification and design

Questions of design and coding have been discussed above in terms of the original data source and the treatment of missing values. It is important to give careful consideration to the coding method used to represent the data and, particularly in this case for the booking data as discussed above, systems and process issues concerning the path the data take from source to final usage. The preliminary selection of variables is another area where decisions taken early in a study can limit the flexibility of choice later in the process of analysing the data and making the results operational. It is important that several different people are involved in discussions on the initial shape of the model, to capture different views, emphases and business interests. Remember that the comparative priority of different variables may change as the study proceeds, and that learnings during the study may require periodic rethinking of the model structure. This is all part of the fact that developing a data mining model on real-world data is an iterative process. Because of the number of different models which may be generated along the way, it is useful to document why particular design decisions were made and to employ some version control, although this tends to be a difficult discipline in practice for those who are keen to drive the modelling forward using each new set of results.

In considering measurement of the overall benefit of the system, there are two approaches. One is to undertake controlled "experiments", defining control groups, measuring the response in the active and control groups, and performing a statistical significance test. The other is to use a response propensity model based on historic data to give a projection of savings and benefits. A useful tool in applying results from this kind of model is the lift chart (variously described as a gains chart or ROC curve, see figure 2) where the response from mailing a certain percentage of the population can be estimated. In the base case with no propensity model, the curve would be a diagonal straight line.

Average cost and benefit figures can then be applied to estimate an overall return. In a direct mailing application, the propensity modelling approach is applicable under the right combination of cost of mailing, return on a response, accuracy of the propensity model, and limits on the number of mailings.

6   Software and hardware support and integration

With the recent and continuing dramatic improvement in computer performance, hardware issues are less pressing, and relative to other processes commonly undertaken on a desktop computer the training of neural networks no longer seems time consuming. It will usually be the case, though, that specialist software will be used for this task, and in a large company this may present special cases in terms of support which are out of the ordinary or not in line with mainstream policy. This can on occasion present difficulties and reduce productivity for the specialist practitioner.

In this instance the way in which the outcome of the data mining has been implemented so far is by means of rules which are generated in a standard environment. The data mining results are combined with elements of domain knowledge and campaign-specific constraints to arrive at queries which directly generate lists of customers for mailing through an existing system. Hence there are no implementation or integration issues to be dealt with. However, looking forward

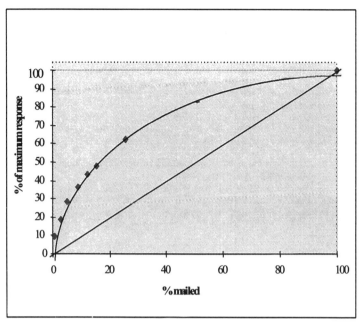

Figure 2: example of lift or gain chart (fictitious data points).

to a time when such a system might be more fully automated and run on a larger scale, the question arises of the best way to "productionise" a data mining set-up. What would be required would be a semi-automated way of turning discoveries from the data into implemented business decisions, and furthermore a way of measuring and tracking such models over time. Such a design would require a model base of potential data mining solutions, combined with some meta-data describing the applicability of the models, some measurement results on the performance of the models and some logic to switch components in and out as required. This would be overseen by a novelty detection or tracking system to spot trends and notify when a particular model was losing performance. These principles are in line with developments in the areas of data warehousing, knowledge management and the application of intelligent software agent methods.

Acknowledgements

The author is grateful to Steven White, Rachel Riley-Snow, Dicken Doe and Amy Stemwedel of British Airways, Tim Bourne, formerly of British Airways and Dr John Pilkington of Scientific Computers Ltd.

References

1. P. Adriaans and D. Zantinge. 1996. *Data Mining* (Addison-Wesley).

2. L. Tarassenko. 1998. *A Guide to Neural Computing Applications*. (Arnold / NCAF).

3. D. Rumelhart and J. McClelland. 1986. *Parallel Distributed Processing*. Vols. I and II, (MIT Press).

4. D.S. Broomhead and D.Lowe. 1988. Multivariable functional interpolation and adaptive networks. *Complex Systems*, **2**, 321-355.

5. J. Moody and C.J. Darken. 1989. Fast learning in networks of locally-tuned processing units. *Neural Computation*, **1**(2), 281-294.

6. C.M. Bishop. 1995. *Neural Networks for Pattern Recognition*. (Oxford University Press).

7. B.D. Ripley. 1996. *Pattern Recognition and Neural Networks*. (Cambridge University Press).

8. Kohonen, T.(1982), "Self-organised formation of topologically correct feature maps", *Biological Cybernetics*, **43**, 59-69.

9. T. Kohonen. 1995. *Self-organizing Maps*, (Springer).

10. Neuralware. 1993. *NeuralWorks Reference Guide*, (Pittsburgh).

Chapter 2

Extracting Rules Concerning Market Segmentation from Artificial Neural Networks

Rudy Setiono
School of Computing
National University of Singapore
Kent Ridge, Singapore 119260
E-mail: rudys@comp.nus.edu.sg

James Y.L. Thong
Department of Information and Systems Management
Hong Kong University of Science and Technology
Clear Water Bay, Hong Kong
E-mail: jthong@ust.hk

Chee-Sing Yap
School of Computing
National University of Singapore
Kent Ridge, Singapore 119260
E-mail: yapcs@comp.nus.edu.sg

1   Introduction

Successful applications of neural network techniques in business research have been widely reported in the literature. Neural networks have been used to predict bank failures[1], to analyse bond rating[2] and audited financial data[3], to assess the financial health of savings and loan associations[4], and to help the planning of end user involvement in the development of information systems[5]. The most attractive feature of neural networks that leads to a wide degree of user acceptance is their high predictive accuracy rate. For some applications such as bank failure prediction, it was reported that neural networks achieve better predictive accuracy than discriminant analysis, logistic regression, k-nearest neighbour, and the decision tree methods.

A major drawback often associated with neural networks as tools for predicting is the lack of 'explanation' capability of trained networks. Although the predictive accuracy of neural networks is often higher than that of other methods or human experts, it is generally difficult to understand *how* a network arrives at a particular conclusion due to the complexity of its architecture. However, it is often desirable to have a set of meaningful and coherent rules that describes under what conditions a pattern will be classified as a member of a certain class. Such rules are a form of knowledge that can be verified by human experts, passed on and expanded. It may also provide a new insight to a problem.

The search for interesting and useful patterns that exist in a data set has spawned the interdisciplinary research area known as data mining. Data mining generally applies some machine learning techniques to achieve its goal of discovering the interesting patterns hidden in the data. Some of the machine learning techniques employed in data mining include inductive methods that build decision trees such as C4.5[6] and CART[7] and clustering algorithms such as the k-nearest neighbour[8] and COBWEB[9]. The use of neural networks as tools for data mining was largely limited due to their lack of explanation capability. Recent developments in algorithms that extract rules from neural networks, however, have made the neural network approach a viable technique for data mining[10].

The objectives of this chapter are twofold: (1) to describe NeuroRule, a system that we have developed to extract decision rules from neural networks[11], and (2) to illustrate the application of NeuroRule as a tool in business research. The application chosen is to distinguish characteristics of organisations using computers. The data for this study have been collected from 638 business organisations in the service sector in the United Kingdom through a mail survey[12].

The chapter is organised as follows. In the next section, we describe NeuroRule and its three main components: a network pruning algorithm, a hidden unit activation clustering algorithm, and a rule extraction algorithm. Following that, we illustrate the NeuroRule approach through a case study of information technology (IT) adoption among service companies in the United Kingdom. We present the results obtained from applying NeuroRule on the 638 survey samples. We will analyse the rules that are extracted to distinguish between organisations using computers and those that are not using them. Finally, we conclude the paper with implications of NeuroRule.

2   Rule extraction with NeuroRule

The process of rule extraction from a neural network can be summarised as follows:

1. Select and train a network to meet the prespecified accuracy requirement.
2. Remove the redundant connections in the network by pruning while maintaining its accuracy.
3. Discretize the hidden unit activation values of the pruned network by clustering.
4. Extract rules that describe the network outputs in terms of the discretized hidden unit activation values.
5. Generate rules that describe the discretized hidden unit activation values in terms of the network inputs.
6. Merge the two sets of rules generated in Steps 4 and 5 to obtain a set of rules that relates the inputs and outputs of the network.

In Step 1, a suitable network is selected and trained for the problem in hand. The network that we use is the standard three-layer feedforward network[13]. Figure 1 depicts such a network. This network can be trained by a simple first-order method like the backpropagation algorithm or a higher-order method such as the Newton-Raphson algorithm[14].

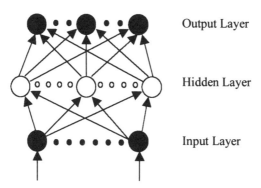

Output Layer

Hidden Layer

Input Layer

Figure 1: A fully connected feedforward neural network with a single hidden layer.

Rules extraction from neural networks can be substantially made easier after the complexity of the network is reduced. Steps 2 and 3 reduce the network complexity and facilitate the process of rule extraction by pruning redundant connections of the network and clustering its hidden unit activation values. The network pruning algorithm is described in more details in the next subsection.

In Step 3, the activation values of a hidden unit are clustered such that only a finite and usually small number of discrete values need to be considered while at the same time maintaining the network accuracy. A small number of different discrete activation values and a small number of connections from the input units to the hidden units will yield a set of compact rules for the data. Finally, Steps 4-6 describe how the rules can be generated.

2.1   Pruning the Neural Network

Step 1 of NeuroRule involves training of a fully connected neural network. Given a set of input-output pairs, the training of the neural network entails finding a set of weights that minimises the network error function. The error function that we minimise is the cross-entropy function:

$$F(w,v) = -\sum_{i=1}^{k}\sum_{p=1}^{C} t_{pi}\log S_{pi} + (1-t_{pi})\log(1-S_{pi}) \tag{1}$$

where:

- k is the number of patterns.
- C is the number of output units.
- $t_{pi} = 0$ or 1 is the target value for the N-dimensional input pattern x_i at output unit p.
- S_{pi} is the output of the network at output unit p for pattern x_i:

$$S_{pi} = \sigma\left(\sum_{m=1}^{H}\alpha_m v_{pm}\right)$$

- $\sigma(\lambda)$ is the sigmoid function $\sigma(\lambda) = 1/(1 + e^{-\lambda})$.
- α_m is the activation value at hidden unit m

$$\alpha_m = \delta(x_i^T w_m + \tau_m)$$

- $x_i^T w_m$ is computed as the scalar product

$$x_i^T w_m = \sum_{j=1}^{N} x_{ij} w_{mj}$$

- $\delta(\lambda)$ is the hyperbolic tangent function $\delta(\lambda) = (e^\lambda - e^{-\lambda})/(e^\lambda + e^{-\lambda})$.
- H is the number of hidden units in the network.
- τ_m is the threshold or bias at hidden unit m.
- w_m is an N-dimensional vector of weights for the arcs connecting the input layer and the m-th hidden unit. The weight of the connection from the j-th input unit to the m-th hidden unit is denoted by w_{mj}.
- v_m is a C-dimensional vector of weights for the arcs connecting the m-th hidden unit and the output layer. The weight of the connection from the m-th hidden unit to the p-th output unit is denoted by v_{pm}.

Experimental results have indicated that the cross-entropy error function (1) enjoys faster convergence than the normal sum of squared errors function[15]. Our implementation applied the BFGS (Broyden-Fletcher-Goldfarb-Shanno) algorithm to minimise this cross-entropy function. The BFGS method, a variant of the quasi-Newton methods has been shown to be superior to the backpropagation method[16].

Step 2 of NeuroRule prunes the redundant connections and units from the trained network. One of the difficulties with using feedforward neural networks is the need to determine the optimal number of hidden units before the training process can begin. Too many hidden units may lead to over-fitting of the data and poor generalisation, while too few hidden units may not produce a network that learns the data well. The step that we have taken to overcome this difficulty is to start with more than the necessary hidden units. Redundant units are subsequently eliminated from the network after the training process has terminated. In order to eliminate irrelevant input units and hidden units, a trained network needs to be trimmed by pruning. The pruning algorithm must be able to identify those connections in the network that are redundant. Removing the redundant connections from the network usually increases the capability of the network to generalise, i.e., to predict new patterns not used for training with a satisfactory accuracy rate. An input unit that has all its connections to the units in the hidden layer removed can be eliminated without affecting the network accuracy. Similarly, a hidden unit that has all its input or output connections eliminated should also be removed from the network.

There are many algorithms for neural network pruning proposed in the past few years[17,18,19]. A pruning algorithm normally requires that a weight-decay term be added to the error function so that connections that are redundant will have weights with small magnitude at the end of training. For each weight w in the network, we add the weight decay term

$$P(w) = \varepsilon_1 \frac{\beta w^2}{(1 + \beta w^2)} + \varepsilon_2 w^2 \qquad (2)$$

where ε_1, ε_2, and β are positive parameters to the error function (1).

Network connections are removed based on their magnitude. The details of the pruning algorithm that makes use of the weight-decay term (2) can be found in

Setiono[18]. The pruning algorithm is shown to be very successful in finding minimal networks for the problems tested.

2.2   Clustering activation values of hidden unit

Step 3 of NeuroRule performs clustering or discretisation of the hidden unit activation values of samples that are correctly classified by the pruned network. Clustering is accomplished by a simple greedy algorithm:

2.2.1   Greedy Clustering Algorithm (GCA)

1. Find the smallest positive integer d such that if all the network activation values are rounded to d decimal-place, the network still retains its accuracy rate.
2. Represent each activation value α by the integer nearest to $\alpha \times 10^d$. Let $H_i = \{h_{i,1}, h_{i,2}, h_{i,3}, \ldots, h_{i,k}\}$ be the set of these representations at hidden unit i for patterns $x_1, x_2, \ldots, x_k$ and let $\vartheta = \{H_1, H_2, \ldots, H_H\}$ be the set of the hidden representations of all patterns at all H hidden units.
3. Set $i=1$.
4. Sort the set ϑ such that the values of H_i are in increasing order.
5. Find a pair of distinct adjacent values $h_{i,j}$ and $h_{i,j+1}$ in the sorted set such that if $h_{i,j+1}$ is replaced by $h_{i,j}$, no conflicting data will be generated.
6. If such a pair of values exists, replace all occurrences of $h_{i,j+1}$ by $h_{i,j}$ and repeat Step 5. Otherwise, set $i = i + 1$.
7. If $i \leq H$, go to Step 4, else Stop.

When the hyperbolic tangent function is used as the hidden unit activation function, the hidden unit activation value of a pattern can take any value in the interval $[-1,1]$. GCA tries to merge as many hidden unit activation values as possible into a single value provided that the merging does not produce conflicting data, i.e., there are two or more identical clustered activation values for patterns that belong to different classes. Steps 1 and 2 of GCA find integer representations of all hidden unit activation values. A small value for d in Step 1 indicates that relatively few distinct activation values are sufficient for the network to maintain its accuracy. For example, when d=2, the distinct values are $-1,-0.99,-0.98,\ldots,0.99,1$. In general, there could be up to $2 \times 10^d + 1$ distinct values. For the results reported here, we set the value of d to 2.

After sorting the activation values according to the values of H_i, pairs of adjacent values are selected for possible merging based on their distance. We implemented Step 5 of the algorithm by first finding a pair of adjacent distinct values with the smallest difference $(h_{i,j+1} - h_{i,j})$. If they can be merged, we replace the larger value with the smaller one. Otherwise, a pair with the second shortest distance will be considered. This process is repeated until there is no more pair of values that can be merged. The next hidden unit will then be considered.

2.3 Extracting rules from the Neural Network

Step 4 of NeuroRule generates rules which relate the clustered activation values with the target values/class labels, while **Step 5** generates rules that relate the activation values with the attribute values at the input units connected to each hidden unit. When the number of clusters in the hidden units is small, it is easy to obtain rules to describe the network outputs in terms of the activation values. Similarly, when the number of inputs connected to a hidden unit is small, it will be trivial to extract rules that describe how each cluster of activation values is obtained from the input values. A general-purpose algorithm X2R[20] was implemented to automate the rule generation process. It takes as input a set of discrete patterns with the class labels and produces the rules describing the relationship between the patterns and their class labels.

X2R produces perfect rules, i.e., it does not introduce misclassifications. Therefore, the error rate of the rules generated is no worse than the inconsistency rate present in the data. Note that the clusters at the hidden units have been computed using those activation values from the correctly classified samples only. Hence, applying X2R to neural network rule extraction, it is always possible to have a zero error rate for both sets of rules from the input layer to the hidden layer and from the hidden layer to the output layer. As a result, the classification accuracy of the rules extracted from a network is at least as high as the accuracy of the network.

Each condition of the rules generated in Step 4 is given in terms of the clustered hidden unit activation values. The rules generated in Step 5 explain how each of the clustered activation values is obtained in terms of the input attributes of the data. Merging of the two sets of rules is achieved by replacing the conditions of the rules from Step 4 with the inputs that describe each activation value obtained from Step 5.

3 Applying NeuroRule to market segmentation

A mail survey was carried out on the service sector in the United Kingdom[12]. Of the 638 returned questionnaires, 443 are from organisations using computers and the rest are from organisation not using them. The service sector was chosen because it is a sector of the economy that has been undergoing rapid changes as a direct result of the information technology revolution. The service sector is further divided into five sub-sectors according to the Standard Industrial Classification (SIC) for the United Kingdom:

- transport and communication
- wholesale distribution
- retail distribution
- business and financial services and
- miscellaneous services including hotels and catering, repairs, and recreational services.

Ten research variables were included based on two main criteria (see Table 1). Firstly, they had been found in previous studies to be relevant to organisational use of computers. Secondly, there must be a simple yet meaningful operational measure that could be incorporated in a mail questionnaire. Descriptions of the variables are given in Appendix A.

Variable	Type	Possible values	Network Inputs
TURNOVER	Ordinal	1,2,3	I_1, I_2, I_3
SECTOR	Nominal	1,2,3,4,5	I_4, I_5, I_6, I_7, I_8
ROCE	Ordinal	1,2,3,4,5	$I_9, I_{10}, I_{11}, I_{12}, I_{13}$
GROW	Ordinal	1,2,3,4,5	$I_{14}, I_{15}, I_{16}, I_{17}, I_{18}$
ROUTINE	Ordinal	1,2,3,4,5	$I_{19}, I_{20}, I_{21}, I_{22}, I_{23}$
PINFO	Continuous	0 – 0.92	I_{24}
FORMAL	Ordinal	1,2,3,4,5	$I_{25}, I_{26}, I_{27}, I_{28}, I_{29}$
CENTRAL	Ordinal	1,2,3,4,5	$I_{30}, I_{31}, I_{32}, I_{33}, I_{34}$
COMPETE	Ordinal	1,2,3,4,5	$I_{35}, I_{36}, I_{37}, I_{38}, I_{39}$
PREDICT	Ordinal	1,2,3,4,5	$I_{40}, I_{41}, I_{42}, I_{43}, I_{44}$

Table 1: Research variables and their network inputs.

One of the ten variables, PINFO, is real-valued. The remaining nine variables have discrete integer values. The possible range for these values is from 1 to 5, except for TURNOVER, which has a possible range from 1 to 3. Before neural network training can start, the raw data need to be pre-processed. PINFO is normalised into the interval [0,1] by dividing all values by the largest value in the data, which is 0.92. The ordinal variables are coded using the thermometer coding scheme[21]. For example, the three possible values of TURNOVER, 1 (indicating turnover of less than £1 million), 2 (indicating turnover between £1 million and £5 million), or 3 (indicating turnover greater than £5 million), are coded as (0,0,1), (0,1,1), and (1,1,1) respectively. Hence, three network inputs are required for this variable. The only nominal discrete variable is SECTOR. The transport, wholesale, retail, banking and finance, and miscellaneous sectors are coded as (1,0,0,0,0),

(0,1,0,0,0), (0,0,1,0,0), (0,0,0,1,0), and (0,0,0,0,1) respectively. The network inputs required for all variables are summarised in Table 1. The table shows how the 10 variables are assigned 44 input units in the network.

Associated with each of the samples is a class label, which takes a value of either 1 or 0 depending on whether the organisation is using or not using computers respectively. An organisation using computers is correctly classified if the network output is greater than or equal to 0.50, while an organisation not using computer is correctly classified if the network output is less than 0.50.

3.1 Results from Neural Network training and pruning

Due to the non-convexity of the error function, the BFGS algorithm may terminate at different local minima of the error function when started from different initial weights. To test the robustness of the training and pruning algorithms, we trained 50 neural networks. Each of these networks has 44 input units, 6 hidden units and 1 output unit. The initial weights of the network connections were generated randomly and uniformly in the interval [-1,1].

Before pruning	
Number of connections	270
Number of hidden units	6
Average accuracy (training set)	84.23% (3.00%)
Average accuracy (cross-validation set)	77.67% (2.63%)
Average accuracy (test set)	78.56% (2.29%)
After pruning	
Number of connections	10.30 (5.24)
Number of hidden units	2.72 (1.16)
Average accuracy (training set)	75.81% (0.61%)
Average accuracy (cross-validation set)	78.72% (2.06%)
Average accuracy (test set)	79.08% (1.69%)

Table 2: Statistics from 50 pruned networks. Note: Figures in parentheses are standard deviations.

The 638 samples were randomly divided into 3 sets. The training set consists of 60% of the total (382 samples), the cross-validation set consists of 20% of the total (128 samples), and the test set consists of the remaining samples. There is a trade-off between the accuracy of the pruned network on the training samples and its complexity. More connections can be removed at the cost of reducing the accuracy of the resulting network. The cross-validation set is used to determine when the pruning process should be terminated. We continued pruning a network as long as its accuracy on the training samples was still at least 75% and its accuracy on the cross-validation samples was within 10% of training accuracy. The results are summarised in Table 2. Note the increase in the average predictive accuracy (accuracy on the test set) and the dramatic decrease in the number of connections after pruning.

4   Extracting rules from pruned networks

After pruning 50 fully connected networks having six hidden units, pruned networks with varying architectures were obtained. The following example is chosen to illustrate how rules are extracted by NeuroRule from a pruned neural network.

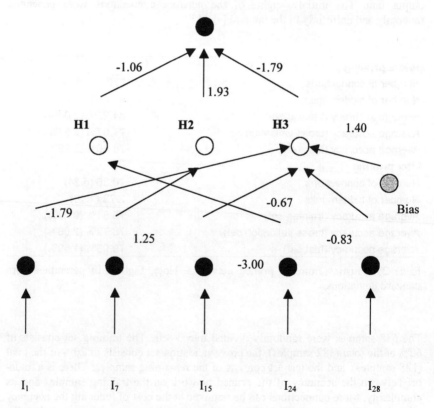

Figure 2: A pruned neural network with three hidden units.

A pruned network that still has the continuous input is shown in Figure 2. The accuracy rates of this network on the training (including cross-validation) and test data sets are 76.08% and 82.03%, respectively. Hidden units 1 and 2 are connected to only one input each, while hidden unit 3 is connected to three input units and has a nonzero bias. After running GCA, we find that there are 2, 2, and 3 clusters respectively at the three hidden units (see Table 3).

Hidden unit	Clusters
1	[-1, -0.84), [-0.84, 1]
2	[0, 0.85), [0.85, 1]
3	[-1, 0.51), [0.51, 0.62), [0.62, 1]

Table 3: The clusters found by GCA for the network shown in Figure 2.

For hidden unit 1, GCA found 2 clusters, that is all activation values in the interval [-1,-0.84) can be replaced by -1 and all activation values in the interval [-0.84,1] can be replaced by -0.84. Representing the pattern by their clustered hidden unit activation values, we found that all 12 possible combinations of the clustered values were present in the training data. Let $\alpha_1 = 1$ or 2 denote the interval in which the first hidden unit activation value of a pattern lies. Similarly, let $\alpha_2 = 1$ or 2, and $\alpha_3 = 1$, 2, or 3 denote the interval at the hidden units 2 and 3 respectively. The rules extracted by X2R in terms of the discretised activation values are as follows:

Rule 1:
- If [$\alpha_2 = 1$ and $\alpha_3 = 3$] OR [$\alpha_1 = 2$ and $\alpha_2 = 1$ and $\alpha_3 = 2$], then not using computer.
- Default rule. Using computer.

We next generate the rules that describe the activation values of the hidden units in terms of their inputs.

Hidden unit 1. The continuous input I_{24} is the only one connected to this hidden unit. The weight of this connection is -3.00. We want to obtain the condition that has to be satisfied by a pattern so that its hidden activation values lies in the interval [-0.84, 1], that is $\alpha_1 = 2$. The condition is as follows:

- If $-3.00\ I_{24} \geq \delta^{-1}(-0.84) = -1.22$, then $\alpha_1 = 2$.
- Default rule. $\alpha_1 = 1$.

Simplifying the conditions of the rules, we obtain:

- If $I_{24} \le 0.41$, then $\alpha_1 = 2$.
- Default rule. $\alpha_1 = 1$.

Hidden unit 2. Only I_7 is connected to this hidden unit. We obtain the simple rule:

- If $I_7 = 0$, then $\alpha_2 = 1$.
- Default rule. $\alpha_2 = 2$.

Hidden unit 3. The 3 binary inputs to these hidden units result in 8 different combinations. We run X2R to generate the rules that determine the various values of α_3. The rules are:

- If $[I_1 = I_{15} = 0$ and $I_{28} = 1]$, then $\alpha_3 = 2$.
- If $[I_1 = I_{28} = 0]$, then $\alpha_3 = 3$.
- Default rule. $\alpha_3 = 1$.

Substituting the rules obtained from the three hidden units into the conditions of Rule 1, we obtain:

Rule 2:

- If $[I_1 = I_7 = I_{28} = 0]$ OR $[I_{24} \le 0.41$ and $I_1 = I_7 = I_{15} = 0$ and $I_{28} = 1]$, then not using computer.
- Default rule. Using computer.

The input I_{24} represents the normalised value of the continuous attribute PINFO. It was computed as PINFO/0.92. Hence, the condition $I_{24} \le 0.41$ is equivalent to PINFO ≤ 0.38. In terms of the original attributes of the data, the rules are:

Rule 3:

- If [TURNOVER < 3 and SECTOR is not Finance and FORMAL = 1] OR [PINFO ≤ 0.38 and TURNOVER < 3 and SECTOR is not Finance and GROW < 4 and FORMAL ≥ 2], then not using computer.
- Default rule. Using computer.

TURNOVER < 3 corresponds to an organization with an annual turnover of not more than £5 million. The variable FORMAL has possible values from 1 to 5 with 1 indicating a very low degree of formality as far as written rules, procedures, and communications in the organization are concerned. The variable GROW also has possible values from 1 to 5. They represent organizations with large contraction, small contraction, no change, small expansion, and large expansion in their business activities over the previous 3 years when the survey was conducted, respectively. Finally, PINFO ≤ 0.38 indicates that not more than 38% of the total workforce in the organization are information workers. The accuracy of this rule is summarised in Table 4.

Sector	Training set	% Correct	Test set	% Correct
Overall	388/510	76.08%	105/128	82.03%
Transport	39/54	72.22%	10/14	71.43%
Wholesale	145/192	75.52%	42/48	87.50%
Retail	81/118	68.64%	21/29	72.41%
Banking & Finance	88/95	92.63%	21/24	87.50%
Miscellaneous	35/51	68.63%	11/13	84.62%

Table 4: Accuracy of the extracted rules.

For comparison purposes, we also analysed the same data set using discriminant analysis, a method commonly applied for decision support. The results are summarised in Table 5. Note that the overall predictive accuracy rate of 76.56% is lower than the average accuracy rate obtained by the neural networks and the accuracy rate of the rules extracted from one of the networks.

Sector	Training set	% Correct	Test set	% Correct
Overall	382/510	74.90%	98/128	76.56%
Transport	40/54	74.07%	11/14	78.57%
Wholesale	142/192	73.96%	34/48	70.83%
Retail	82/118	69.49%	22/29	75.86%
Banking & Finance	82/95	86.32%	20/24	83.33%
Miscellaneous	36/51	70.59%	11/13	84.62%

Table 5. Accuracy rates from discriminant analysis.

5 Conclusion

Neural networks have been applied widely as tools for decision support. Due to their complex non-linear mapping of the data, neural networks are often viewed as unfathomable black boxes. Previously, it was very difficult to articulate the decision process of a trained network. Having explicit rules that explain the network outcomes can be beneficial in many ways. Explicit rules make it possible for the decision process to be verified by human experts. They may also provide new insight into the problem domain by discovering interesting patterns buried in the data.

This chapter describes a system that extracts decision rules from neural networks. The system is illustrated through an application to identify characteristics of organisations using computers in the service sector in the United Kingdom. Three factors enable us to extract a compact set of rules from neural networks that classify the samples with high accuracy. The first factor is a very effective neural network pruning algorithm. By using a penalty function, we are able to prune networks such that only very few input units, hidden units and connections remained. The second factor is an algorithm that clusters hidden unit activation values of a pruned network. This algorithm allows us to consider only a small number of different hidden unit activation values and still maintain the accuracy of the original network. The third factor is X2R, an algorithm that generates classification rules from small data sets having discrete inputs. The rules extracted from the neural networks achieved higher predictive accuracy than discriminant analysis. They can be used to identify specific segments of the service sector for promotion of IT adoption. The system to extract rules from neural networks presented here is general and can be applied to other business applications where neural networks may profitably be used for classification and prediction.

References

1. K.Y. Tam and K.Y. Kiang. 1992. Managerial applications of neural networks: the case of bank failure predictions. *Management Science*, **38**(7), 926-947.

2. S. Dutta, S. Shekhar and W.Y. Wong. 1994. Decision support in non-conservative domains: generalization with neural networks. *Decision Support Systems*, **11**(5), 527-544.

3. J.R. Coakley and C.E. Brown. 1993. Artificial neural networks applied to ratio analysis in the analytical review process. *Intelligent Systems in Accounting, Finance and Management*, **2**, 19-39.

4. L.M. Salchenberger, E.M. Cinar and N.A. Lash. 1992. Neural networks: a new tool for predicting thrift failures. *Decision Sciences*, **23**(4), 899-916.

5. R.W. Lodewyck and P.S. Deng. 1993. Experimentation with a backpropagation neural network-an application to planning end user system development. *Information & Management*, **24**, 1-8.

6. J.R. Quinlan. 1993. *C4.5: Programs for Machine Learning*. (San Francisco, CA: Morgan Kaufmann)

7. L. Breiman, J.H. Friedman, R.A. Olshen and C.J. Stone. 1984. *Classification and Regression Trees*. (Belmont, CA: Wadsworth International Group)

8. T.M. Cover and P.E. Hart. 1967. Nearest neighbour pattern classification. *IEEE Transactions on Information Theory*, **IT-13**, 21-27.

9. D.H. Fisher. 1987. Knowledge acquisition via incremental conceptual clustering. *Machine Learning*, 2(7), 139-172.

10. H. Lu, R. Setiono and H. Liu. 1996. Effective data mining using neural networks. *IEEE Transactions on Knowledge and Data Engineering*, 8(6), 957-961.

11. R. Setiono and H. Liu. 1996. Symbolic representation of neural networks. *IEEE Computer*, 71-77.

12. C.S. Yap. 1990. Distinguishing characteristics of organisations using computers. *Information & Management*, 18, 97-107.

13. D.E. Rumelhart and K. McClelland (Eds.). 1986. *Parallel Distributed Processing: Explorations in Microstructure of Cognition*, Vols. 1-2, (MIT Press)

14. S. Piramuthu, M.J. Shaw and J.A. Gentry. 1994. A classification approach using multi-layer neural-networks. *Decision Support Systems*, 11(5), 509-526.

15. A. van Ooyen and B. Nienhuis. 1992. Improving the convergence of the backpropagation algorithm. *Neural Networks*, 5, 465-471.

16. R. Setiono and L.C.K. Hui. 1995. Use of quasi-newton method in a feedforward neural network construction algorithm. *IEEE Transactions on Neural Networks*, 6(1), 273-277.

17. E.D. Karnin. 1990. A simple procedure for pruning backpropagation trained neural networks. *IEEE Transactions on Neural Networks*, 1(2), 239-242.

18. R. Setiono. 1997. A penalty-function approach to pruning feedforward neural networks. *Neural Computation*, 9(1), 185-204.

19. H.H. Thodberg. 1991. Improving Generalisation of Neural Networks Through Pruning. *Int. Journal of Neural Systems*, 1(4), 317-326.

20. H. Liu and S.T. Tan. 1995. X2R: A fast rule generator. In *Proceedings of IEEE International Conference on Systems, Man and Cybernetics*, (New York: IEEE Press), 388-391.

21. M. Smith. 1993. *Neural Networks for Statistical Modeling*. (Van Nostrand Reinhold)

Appendix A. Description of research variables.

Variable	Description
TURNOVER	Annual turnover
SECTOR	Industrial sector
ROCE	Average return on capital over the last 3 years
GROW	Growth of business over the last 3 years
ROUTINE	Routineness of work activities
PINFO	Percentage of information workers
FORMAL	Degree of formalisation of communications
CENTRAL	Degree of centralisation of decision making
COMPETE	Competitiveness of the market
PREDICT	Predictability of customer's requirements

Chapter 3

Characterising and Segmenting the Business-to-Consumer E-Commerce Market Using Neural Networks

A. Vellido and P.J.G. Lisboa
School of Computing and Mathematical Sciences, Liverpool John Moores University.
Byrom St. Liverpool L3 3AF, UK
E-mail: a.vellido@livjm.ac.uk
http://www.cms.livjm.ac.uk/research/snc/neural.htm

K. Meehan
Business School, Liverpool John Moores University.
Mount Pleasant. Liverpool L3 5UZ
E-mail: k.meehan@livjm.ac.uk

1   Introduction

Business-to-consumer electronic commerce is deemed to have considerable market potential for the future, fuelled by the size of the worldwide market resulting from the exponential growth of Internet adoption. Realizing this full potential requires a careful identification of the online customers' needs and expectations. Public organizations such as the European Association for the Co-ordination of Consumer Representation in Standardization (ANEC) are already trying to promote standardization of online transaction protocols, based on consumers' opinions, in order to sustain the e-commerce growth[1].

Research on Internet consumer behaviour is still in its infancy, and most of the published studies in the area are exploratory and qualitative. A quantitative framework for the analysis of consumers' online shopping behaviour is yet to be provided. This chapter proposes such a quantitative framework, structured in several stages:

- Characterization of the Internet users opinions of online shopping, using factor analysis.
- Selection of the factors which are predictive of the propensity to buy online using logistic regression and neural network-based techniques.
- Classification of the Internet users into the groups of online purchasers and non-purchasers, using linear discriminant analysis, logistic regression and neural network models, according to the factors selected by the aforementioned techniques.
- Segmentation of the online market using a statistically principled neural network-based model: the Generative Topographic Mapping (GTM)[2]

The first three stages will provide a parsimonious latent description of the Internet user opinions of on-line shopping, in the form of factors proven to be predictive of the propensity to buy on-line. This description should ease the design and implementation of information-based marketing strategies in a medium characterized by the overabundance of data. Cluster-based market segmentation, the fourth stage in this framework, has recently been cited as the most important use of data mining in the context of Internet retailing[3].

Overall, the formulation of a general quantitative framework for the analysis of online consumer behaviour will yield a sound empirical basis for business decision making.

This chapter is organized in sections corresponding to each of the four stages of the quantitative methodology described above.

2   The latent dimensions underlying the Internet users' opinions of online shopping

In this section, the real-world data used in the study are described, including a brief outline of the rationale behind the application of factor analysis and a presentation of results, interpreted according to existing literature.

2.1   Description of the data used in this study

This study is based upon publicly available data from the web-based 9th GVU's WWW User Survey[4]. From the first two questions of its "Internet Shopping (Part 1) Questionnaire" ("general opinion of using the WWW for shopping as compared to other means of shopping" and "opinion of Web-based vendors compared to vendors in other forms of shopping"), 44 items were selected (to be identified, from this point, as data set A). These items were complemented with information on age, household income, years of Internet experience, and average of hours a week of Internet usage (These four variables to be identified as data set B). The dependent variable used for the variable selection and classification experiments in section 3 is binary in nature and responds to the question of whether the respondent has or has not ever purchased online. This will divide the data set into the classes of purchasers and non-purchasers. The original data sample of 2180 individuals was not balanced in terms of class membership. Several class-balanced data sets are created for some of the experiments in the next sections.

2.2 Factor analysis rationale and methodology

The modeling of data in high dimensional spaces is likely to be affected by problems of curse of dimensionality and overfitting (leading to a lack of generalizability of the models). Furthermore, the results of the analyses based on a parsimonious description of the data, stemming from the dimensionality reduction procedures, are expected to be more interpretable and operational in managerial terms. There are two main approaches to overcome this potential problem: either the selection of a subset of the original, observable variables, or the generation of a group of new variables, non-observable or latent, as a combination of the original ones[5]. Factor analysis follows the latter approach. The factor analysis of the data can be further justified on the basis of the following arguments[6]:

- It can help to overcome some of the limitations associated with survey data: Presence of noise, poorly measured variables, inadequate selection of survey items in terms of balance across studied constructs.
- The resulting factor structure can be interpreted in terms that are not explicit in the observable data, and becomes more applicable in the business context.

The factor extraction was accomplished using the Maximum Likelihood method, as it is the only systematic and theoretically sound procedure capable of producing a generalised likelihood ratio test of goodness of fit[7] that can be used as a guidance for the selection of the number of factors of the final model. The factors were rotated using the *Varimax* procedure to a final orthogonal structure. It is generally agreed that where a simple structure with orthogonal factors can be found, this is the most efficient method. The Kaiser-Meyer-Olkin (KMO) measures of sampling adequacy fall between the categories of "middling" and "meritorious", according to the ranks devised by Kaiser[8]; the validity of the factor model is therefore supported.

2.3 Factor analysis results and their interpretation

The interpretation of the factor analysis results always conveys a certain degree of subjectivity. Comparing the quantitative results to previously published qualitative studies on factors influencing online shopping adoption can alleviate this potential shortcoming.

Review of the literature on factors influencing online shopping

In a recent study based on an open-ended survey, Jarvenpaa and Todd[9] described a salient structure for attitudes towards online shopping. It consisted of four main groups of factors, inspired by traditional retail patronage, and adapted to the Web shopping context. These groups of factors can be summarized as:

- **Product perceptions**, including the dimensions of *price, quality* and *variety*. Given that the marketing concept of product is rapidly evolving and becoming increasingly information-based[10], a further dimension to those described in Jarvenpaa and Todd[9] (but also coming out as an unexpected salient factor in that study) is the *information richness* of products. It can be associated to the problem of their lack of *tangibility*.

- **Shopping experience**, described as a mixture of *effort, compatibility* and *playfulness*. In the online context, effort is more mental than physical, and can involve ease of use and ease of placing and cancelling orders. *Compatibility* refers to the consumers' lifestyle and shopping habits. Finally, *playfulness* can be described in the Internet context, by making use of the flow construct[11].

- **Customer service** includes *responsiveness, assurance, reliability, tangibility* and *empathy*. *Responsiveness* "concerns how well prepared merchants are to meet the diverse needs of shoppers during the different phases of shopping". *Assurance* is "the degree to which the service provider instils confidence in customers". *Reliability* is "the degree to which the service provider can be counted on to deliver on his or her promises". The concept of *tangibility* refers to the ability of the vendor to replace the real product with an information-rich substitute. Finally, *empathy* is defined as the degree to which the vendor is able to adapt to the individual needs of the consumer.

- **Consumer risk** is split into *economic, social, performance* and *personal* risks. The *economic risk* "stems from the possibility of monetary loss associated with buying a product". *Personal risk* has to be understood in terms of the concept of environmental control[12]. *Performance risk* involves the "perception that a product or service may fail to meet expectations". Finally, *Social risk* is concerned with both the consumer's self-perception, and that of their peers.

In another important study, Hoffman et al.[12] described, from the point of view of consumers' information privacy concerns, some other factors that could influence online shopping adoption: *environmental control* and *secondary use of information control*.

- *Environmental control* is defined as the "consumer's ability to control the actions of other people in the environment during a market transaction". It implies security and economic risk and it is proportional to the level of anonymity.
- *Secondary use of information control* is defined as "the consumer's ability to control the dissemination of information related to or provided during such transactions or behaviours to those who were not present".

The findings of these mainly qualitative studies are to be used as a benchmark for the identification and description of the factors stemming from the experiments in *section 3.*

Presentation of the results

The generalized likelihood ratio test of goodness of fit suggested a 9-factor solution for the *data set A*. It is summarized in *table 1* and interpreted as follows:

- **Factor 1** is general in terms of loading variables, but has a definite interpretation as shopping experience, in terms of compatibility, control over the shopping experience, and convenience.
- **Factor 2** is very homogeneous and refers to consumer risk perception from the point of view of environmental control: perceptions of trust and security are involved.
- **Factor 3** turns out in the shape of customer service, along the dimensions of responsiveness and empathy; emphasis is placed on the information richness provided by the vendor, which also relates to aspects of product perception.
- **Factor 4** is undoubtedly perception of affordability, concerning the expense associated with equipment, connection, etc.
- **Factor 5** loads in items that describe effort as ease of use within the shopping experience dimension. Interestingly, further reductions of the factor model (not reported in this study) indicate that this factor would merge with factor 4, revealing correlation between the perceptions of economic effort and user effort.
- **Factor 6** complements factor 3, as it focuses on information richness in terms of the product perception of variety.
- **Factor 7** mixes the concepts of assurance and reliability in customer service with the perception of performance risk.
- **Factor 8** also concerns consumer risk but from the point of view of the consumers' image, and could be labelled as elitism.
- **Factor 9** addresses another aspect of the shopping experience: Effort associated to the vendors' performance; it is, thus, related to responsiveness and empathy.

2.4   Summary

The factor analysis experiment has demonstrated the existence of a parsimonious latent structure underlying Internet users' opinions of, online shopping, explainable in meaningful, marketing-operative terms. This latent structure is consistent, in terms of interpretation, with the findings of previous qualitative studies[9,12]. The application of factor analysis is expected to help to overcome some of the limitations associated with survey-based studies: noisy data, poorly measured variables based on subjective ratings, and unbalanced item selection across the domain of the surveyed constructs.

FACTOR	DESCRIPTION	ATTRIBUTES
1	Shopping experience: Compatibility	Control and convenience
2	Consumer risk perception / Environmental control	Trust and security
3	Customer service	Responsiveness and empathy/ Information richness
4	Affordability	--
5	Shopping experience: Effort	Ease of use
6	Product perception	Variety: Information richness
7	Customer service / Consumer risk	Assurance and reliability / Performance risk
8	Consumer risk: Image risk	Elitism
9	Shopping experience / Customer service	Effort / Responsiveness and empathy

Table 1: Descriptive summary of the factor structure

3   Prediction of the propensity to buy from the Internet channel

In this section, we intend to answer to the following questions:

- *Question 1*: Which of the factors in table 1 contain the necessary information to best predict Web users' online purchasing behaviour? Are commonly used variables, such as age, household income, and Web usage patterns, good predictors of this behaviour?
- *Question 2*: To what extent can online purchasing behaviour be inferred, using linear discriminant analysis (LDA), logistic regression (LR) and neural network methods, from a selection of the latent factors shown to be the best predictors of such behaviour?

3.1 Variable selection

3.1.1 Quantitative variable selection in the electronic commerce literature

Linear regression was used in Jarvenpaa and Todd[9] to relate four main salient factors constitutive of online shopping behaviour with two dependent variables: *attitudes toward shopping* and *intention toward shopping*. It was concluded that *attitudes* were significantly influenced by *product perception, shopping experience* and *consumer risk*, but not by *customer service*. On the other hand, *intention* was shown to be influenced by *product perception, shopping experience* and *customer service* but not by *consumer risk*. Demographic and socio-economic variables were shown not to be related to the dependent variable of *attitudes toward shopping*.

3.1.2 Variable selection model: Automatic Relevance Determination for Bayesian Neural Networks

Neural Networks are frequently considered as *black boxes* due to their supposed incapacity to identify the relevance of independent variables in non-linear terms. Nevertheless, in recent years this potential drawback has been addressed. This study resorts to a statistically sound and non-linear in nature method: Automatic Relevance Determination (ARD) for supervised Bayesian Neural Networks[13]. Within the basic Bayesian approach, the weight decay or regularization term that helps to control the complexity of the network can be interpreted as a Gaussian prior distribution over the network parameters (weights and biases), of the form

$$p(\mathbf{w}) = A \exp\left(-\alpha \sum_{i}^{W} w_i^2 / 2\right), \qquad (1)$$

where $\mathbf{w} = \{w_i\}$ is the vector of network parameters, W is the total number of network parameters, and A is the inverse of a normalization factor. Instead, the ARD model associates an individual regularization term to each group of network parameters. The weights between each input and the hidden layer are grouped separately, and two extra groups (bias to the hidden nodes and weights plus bias to the output) are considered. Therefore, the prior over the weights becomes

$$p(\mathbf{w}) = A \exp\left(-\sum_c^C \alpha_c \sum_i^{W_c} w_{ci}^2 / 2 \right) \tag{2}$$

where C = (number of inputs + 2) is the number of groups, and W_c is the number of parameters in group c, so that $\sum_c^C W_c = W$. As a result of the network training, high α_c values will squash down the weights connected to the corresponding input, and its contribution to the overall model will be diminished. On the contrary, relevant inputs are expected to be associated with relative big weights i.e. low α_c values. Therefore, direct inspection of the final $\{\alpha_c\}$ values will indicate the relative relevance of each variable.

3.1.3 Selection of the most predictive latent variables: Results

The 9-factor scores set plus the variables from *Data set B* (as described in *section 2.1*, including *age, household income,* and *web usage patterns*), are analyzed using the neural network model described above. The results of the ARD procedure indicate that the *Consumer risk perception/Environmental control* factor appears neatly as the main predictor, followed by *Shopping experience: Compatibility; Affordability; Shopping experience / Customer service* and finally *Shopping experience: Effort.* These five factors (According to *table 1*, factors 2, 1, 4, 9 and 5) will be selected for the next experiments. The inclusion of *Customer Service / Consumer Risk* in this selected subset might also be justified. On the other hand *Consumer risk: Image risk* appears to exert no influence whatsoever in the purchasing behaviour. None of the variables in *data set B* turns out to be a good predictor: *household income,* in particular, exerts no discriminatory power.

3.2   Quantitative prediction of online purchasing behaviour

Several inference models are now employed to quantitatively predict propensity to buy online, using the 5-factor selection described in the previous paragraph. The goal is the discrimination of two classes, made up by those who have ever purchased online and those who never have. The classification results are presented using the Receiver Operating Characteristic (ROC) plots of *sensitivity* against *specificity,* plus overall *accuracy.* Sensitivity (true positive fraction) and specificity (true negative fraction) are defined as:

SENSITIVITY = TP / (TP + FN);   SPECIFICITY = TN / (TN + FP) (3)

where TP stands for true positives (individuals predicted to be purchasers who actually are purchasers), TN for true negatives (correctly predicted to be non-purchasers), FP for false positives (incorrectly predicted to be purchasers), and FN for false negatives (incorrectly predicted to be non-purchasers). Accuracy is defined as the overall percentage of correctly classified individuals. These plots offer not just overall classification results but also information about the partial results for each class, which becomes especially important in the case of class-unbalanced samples. Moreover, they inform of the effect of different classification thresholds in the classification performance. The area under the ROC plot (AURP) is a measure of the overall effectiveness of the model in separating the two classes. A measure of 0.5 indicates no separation capabilities, whereas a measure of 1 indicates perfect separation. For detailed information on the use of the ROC plots, see Bradley[14].

3.2.1 5-factor selection: Comparison of LDA, LR, and Neural Network performances

The 5-factor selection (factors 2, 1, 4, 9 and 5, in table 1) is used to compare the predictive capabilities of three inference models: linear discriminant analysis, logistic regression and Bayesian neural networks. The latter is used in two variants: with a single regularization term (SRT), and applying Automatic Relevance Determination (ARD). Their performance is measured by means of the ROC and Accuracy plots, shown in *figure 1*. The behaviour of each of the models will be further illustrated by a detailed inspection of the differences between expected and predicted outputs across the range spanned by some of the variables.

- **Linear Discriminant Analysis**: A test accuracy of 80% is achieved in a leave-one-out procedure. This value is not a function of a decision threshold as in the case of Logistic Regression and the Neural Networks. For the same reason there is no ROC plot associated.
- **Logistic Regression**: A maximum of 80.36% test accuracy is reached at threshold 0.49. The AURP for the test data, summarized in table 2, indicating the probability of correctly ranking two randomly selected individuals, one from the population of online purchasers and one from the population of non-purchasers, is 87.46%.
- **Bayesian Neural Networks**: The SRT model has a maximum accuracy of 81.26% for a threshold of 0.4. The AURP for the test data is 88.02%. The ARD model achieves the same test accuracy of 81.26% but, in this case, for a threshold of 0.48. The AURP for the test data is 88.07%.

Logistic Regression	0.8746
Bayesian MLP (SRT)	0.8802
Bayesian MLP (ARD)	0.8807

Table 2: AURP test measures for the neural network and logistic regression models.

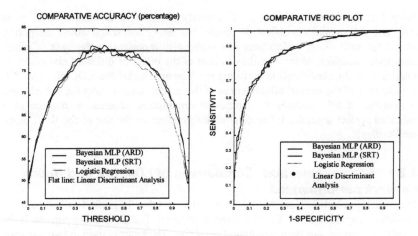

Figure 1: Accuracy plot (left) and ROC plot (right) summarizing the comparative performance of two neural networks (ARD and SRT), logistic regression and linear discriminant analysis. Each of the 101 points shaping the curves corresponds (left to right for the accuracy, right to left for the ROC) to a different classification threshold from 0 to 1, in 0.01 intervals.

These results reveal that there is only a marginal advantage to be obtained from the application of supervised neural networks to these data, both in terms of the overall and the group-specific classifications. It might be argued that the pre-processing of the data (the factor analysis) is likely to have removed most of the non-linearities present in the raw observable data. Some further interesting results can be obtained from a detailed inspection, across the input range, of the models predictions: Figure 2, concerning the factor/variable Shopping Experience: Convenience, shows how the main difference between the predictions of the Linear Discriminant Analysis and Logistic Regression, on one hand, and the Bayesian Neural Networks, on the other, is the way in which the latter manage to predict more accurately those cases at the extremes of the input range. This result was expected, as neural networks are known to be an appropriate model to handle outliers.

3.2.2   The effect of marginalization of the Bayesian Neural Network predictions

Within the Bayesian approach to the training of multi-layer perceptrons for classification problems, the interpretation of the outputs as posterior probabilities of class-membership requires to integrate out (marginalize) the network function over the distribution of network weights. MacKay[15] suggests an approximation of such analytically intractable integral, in which the integration is over the network output preactivations. The network predictions can be overoptimistic if

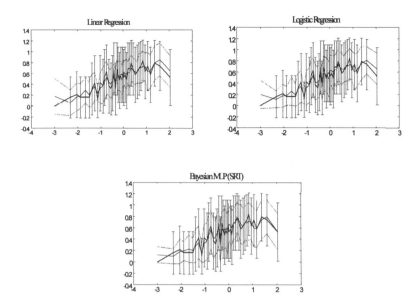

Figure 2: Prediction of the three inference models against the spread of values of the *Shopping Experience: Convenience* factor. The thick solid line and the solid vertical bars correspond, in turn, to the average of the observed class-membership (0 or 1) across the range of the factor values and its standard deviation. The thin solid line and the dashed line correspond, in turn, to the average model prediction and its standard deviation. The closer the two solid lines and the closer the thin solid and the dashed lines, the better the model prediction.

this process of marginalization is ignored. We attempt to assess the effect of marginalization, with the approximation aforementioned, on the Bayesian neural network: Only the results for the model with single regularization term are shown. The expected effect of the marginalization is the *moderation* of the test outputs, as their values are pushed towards 0.5. Should the classification threshold be set to that value, there would be no change in the classification decision.

The ROC plot describing the neural network performance for the SRT model is shown in *figure 3*. The results for the non-marginalized test outputs have already been shown in previous sections. By effect of the marginalization of the test network outputs, the sensitivity values worsen for thresholds over 0.5, whereas the specificity values improve; for thresholds under that value it is the other way around. The discrimination capabilities of the model are assessed by the AURP measure, which is not affected by the marginalization of the test: 88.02% in the case of non-marginalized outputs, and 88.01% in the case of marginalized outputs. The classification results are also summarized in *figure 3*: the model with marginalized outputs achieves an accuracy of over 80% within the threshold interval from 0.39 to 0.51, with a maximum of 81.13% for a threshold of 0.41. The accuracy for a threshold of 0.5 remains unchanged. The effect of the marginalization of the test outputs on the accuracy results is barely noticeable.

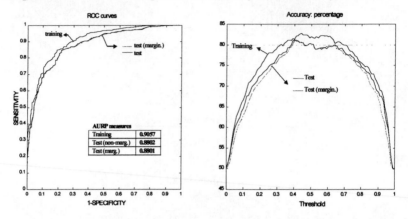

Figure 3: Accuracy plot (right) and ROC plot (left) describing the performance of a SRT Bayesian neural network. The test curves for marginalized and non-marginalized outputs are the result of a 10-fold cross-validation process. Each of the 101 points shaping the curves corresponds (left to right for the accuracy, right to left for the ROC) to a different classification threshold from 0 to 1, in 0.01 intervals.

3.3   Summary

The three questions put forward at the onset of this section have been answered. Consumer risk perception/Environmental control, Shopping experience: Compatibility, Affordability, Shopping experience/Customer service, and Shopping experience: Effort, have been shown to be good predictors of the propensity to buy online. On the other hand, none of the variables in data set B (Household income, age, Years of Internet experience, and Average of hours a week of Internet usage) turned out to be a good predictor, which agrees with the results in Jarvenpaa and Todd[9].

All the inference models have been capable of predicting online purchasing behaviour to a satisfactory degree of accuracy, making use of the 5-factor selection. This parsimonious description of online customers' opinions, drawn from the original 48 observable variables, and explainable in meaningful, operative terms, should be of practical managerial value. It has been shown that, in comparison to other traditional statistical models, only a marginal advantage is to be obtained from the application of supervised neural networks to these data. Nevertheless, neural networks performed better in the identification of outliers. The marginalization of the predictions of the Bayesian neural network model did not harm its performance and yet it provided a "lower bound" that ensures that the network predictions are not overoptimistic.

4 Segmentation of the e-commerce consumer market

The interactive nature of the Internet entails a readjustment of the relationship between marketers and customers. The latter are empowered by the information richness of the medium, which enables unprecedented availability of access to most aspects of the shopping process. In this new commercial framework, where online vendors have to struggle to differentiate their offer and attract the online browsers towards their electronic outlets, market segmentation techniques, grounded on the benefits sought by the customers, can give the marketer a leading edge. The identification of such segments can be the basis for effective targeting, enabling the redirection of made-to-measure content towards the customer. In the context of Internet retailing, the identification of clusters of consumer types has been stated as "the most important use of data mining, as this type of information is useful in a myriad of other planning and development tasks"[3].

There have been recent calls for the design and deployment of market segmentation models grounded in a sound statistical framework[16]. In this section we present one such model, the Generative Topographic Mapping (GTM)[17,18]. Devised as a principled alternative to the well-known Self-Organizing Map[19,20], it retains the visualization capabilities of the SOM whilst overcoming most of its limitations. The GTM is able to accommodate segmentation strategies of different *granularity*, from micro-segmentation to the traditional aggregate segmentation. The existence of a well-defined posterior probability of cluster/segment membership for each individual also makes the GTM a fuzzy clustering tool.

4.1 Description of the data

This section makes use of the same data from the web-based *9th GVU's WWW User Survey* previously described. As explained in section 2, those data were subjected to factor analysis for dimensionality reduction. The nine factor model obtained underwent a process of latent variable selection, and the five factors, described in *section 3.1.3*, shown to be more predictive of the propensity to buy online are the ones to be used in this segmentation study.

4.2   The GTM as a principled model for data visualization and market segmentation

The Generative Topographic Mapping (GTM) is a non-linear latent variable model that generates a probability density in the multi-dimensional data space, using a set of latent variables of smaller dimension. This non-linear mapping is described by the generalized linear regression model

$$y = W\phi(u),$$ (4)

where u is an L-dimensional vector of latent variables, W is the matrix that generates the explicit mapping from latent space to an L-dimensional manifold embedded in data space, and ϕ is a set of R basis functions which, in this study, are chosen to be Gaussians. For the non-linear mapping to remain analytically and computationally tractable, and also to elaborate a principled alternative to the Self-Organizing Map (SOM), the prior distribution of u in latent space is defined as a discrete grid, similar in spirit to the grid of the SOM

$$p(u) = \frac{1}{M} \sum_{i=1}^{M} \delta(u - u_i) \ ,$$ (5)

where M is the number of its nodes. Since the data do not necessarily lie in an L-dimensional space, it is necessary to make use of a noise model for the distribution of data vectors. The integration of this data distribution over the latent space distribution gives

$$p(x|W,\beta) = \int p(x|u,W,\beta)p(u)du \ =$$

$$= \frac{1}{M} \sum_{i=1}^{M} \left(\frac{\beta}{2\pi}\right)^{\frac{D}{2}} \exp\left\{-\frac{\beta}{2}\|m_i - x\|^2\right\}$$ (6)

where D is the dimensionality of the input space, and $m_i = W\phi(u_i)$ for the discrete node representation, according to (4). Using the SOM terminology, m_i can be considered as *reference vectors*, each of them the centre of an isotropic Gaussian distribution in data space[18]. The log-likelihood can now be defined as

$$L(W,\beta) = \sum_{n=1}^{N} \ln p(x^n|W,\beta)$$ (7)

for the whole input data set $\{x^n\}$. The distribution (6) corresponds to a constrained Gaussian mixture model[21], hence its parameters, W and β, can be determined using the Expectation-Maximization (EM) algorithm[22], details of which can be found in Bishop et al.[17]. As part of the Expectation step, the mapping from latent space to data space, defined by (4), can be inverted using Bayes' theorem so that the posterior probability of a GTM node i, given a data-space point is defined as

$$
R_i^n = \frac{\exp\left[-\frac{\beta}{2}\left\|\mathbf{m}_i - \mathbf{x}^n\right\|^2\right]}{\sum_{i'}^{M}\exp\left[-\frac{\beta}{2}\left\|\mathbf{m}_{i'} - \mathbf{x}^n\right\|^2\right]}
\tag{8}
$$

This is known as the *responsibility* taken by each node i for each point n in the data space. Each of the nodes in latent space can be interpreted, as it is for the SOM model[23], as a cluster or, in the context of market segmentation, as a segment. Therefore, equation (8) defines a posterior probability of cluster membership for each cluster and each data point. This is a statistically principled alternative to the *response surfaces* defined for the SOM model[24], based on the quantization error measure. Therefore, and unlike the SOM, the GTM can be properly used as a *fuzzy-clustering* tool.

This well-defined posterior probability will be especially useful for data visualization. The mapping defined by (4) generates a *topographic ordering*: any two points that are close in latent space will be mapped to points that are necessarily close in data space. Consequently, neighbouring clusters in latent space correspond to groups of data that are also close in data space. This preservation of the topographic order will permit, besides the definition of each node in latent space as a cluster / segment, these nodes to be aggregated in a principled way to form macro-clusters. The definition of these macro-clusters can be assisted by the visualization of the *magnification factors*[25]: a measure of the extent to which the vectors in the latent visualization map are stretched in their mapping to data space. The probabilistic formulation of the GTM makes it possible to define this measure as the Jacobian of the transformation between both spaces. Again, this can only be approximated in the SOM model by the visualization of distances between code-book vectors[26].

4.3 Experiments

Now we give a brief account of the implementation of the GTM, followed by the presentation and discussion of the segmentation results.

4.3.1 Implementation of the GTM model

The complexity of the mapping generated by the GTM model is mainly controlled by the number and form of the basis functions. Further control of this effective complexity can be achieved with the addition of a regularization term to the error function (7), in such a way that the training of the GTM would consist of the maximization of a *penalized* log-likelihood

$$L_{PEN}(\mathbf{W},\beta) = \sum_{n=1}^{N} \ln p(\mathbf{x}_n | \mathbf{W},\beta) + \frac{1}{2}\alpha \|\mathbf{w}\|^2, \tag{9}$$

where $\mathbf{w}$ is a vector shaped by concatenation of the different column vectors of the weight matrix $\mathbf{W}$ and α is a real-valued regularization coeficient. This regularization term is effectively preventing the GTM to fit the noise in the data and is used under the assumption that there exist an underlying data generator which is a combination of the density functions for each of the segments. Given that the GTM is formulated within a probabilistic framework, the optimum values for the regularization coefficient α and for the inverse variance of the noise model β can be evaluated using the Bayesian formalism.

The model by which we illustrate the use of the GTM consists of a grid of 5x5 basis functions with a common width $\sigma = 1$. The GTM was trained with a class-balanced data set of 778 individuals and, for the trained single regularization term model, the final values for the regularization coefficient and the inverse variance of the noise model were, in turn, $\alpha = 1.12$ and $\beta = 1.57$. A fixed grid in latent space of 15x15 nodes was selected as a compromise on the level of detail or *granularity* of the cluster / segment solution.

4.3.2 Segmentation results

The equation (8) provides a posterior probability of cluster/segment membership for each individual. In order to visualize that probability for a complete set of data, the information has to be summarized. This can be done[17], in the way that is usual with the SOM model, by calculating the *mode* of the distribution,

$$i^{max} = \arg\max_{\{i\}} R_{in} \tag{10}$$

Class discrimination

We first attempt to visualize to what extent the GTM has managed to separate the classes of *purchasers* and *non-purchasers* as defined in *section 2.1*. It should indicate whether these classes are naturally separated in the data set. *Figure 4* represents the whole data set by the *mode* (8), as mapped into the trained GTM. Each individual has been assigned a colour, black or white, depending on its *true* class membership. Grey nodes indicate that individuals from different classes have been mapped into them. *Figure 1(a)* shows that the GTM, *without any prior information on class membership* has managed to separate, quite clearly, the classes of *purchasers* and *non-purchasers*.

(a)   **(b)**

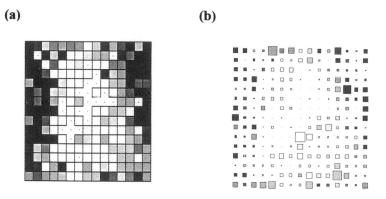

Figure 4: GTM class-membership maps. All the individuals in the training sample are mapped onto the nodes in the latent visualization space that correspond to their *modes* as defined by (10): a) Each individual has been shaded according to its class-membership: white for *purchasers*, black for *non-purchasers*. Those GTM nodes with more than one pattern mapped onto them are depicted in shades of grey, corresponding to the class-membership proportion. The nodes with no individuals mapped onto them are depicted as dots. b) The same pseudo-colour representation has been used, but now the relative size of the squares/nodes corresponds to the number of patterns mapped onto them. Regions of high pattern occurrence in latent space can thus be visualized.

Figure 4(b) conveys information about the size of each of the nodes / micro-clusters (number of individuals whose *mode* corresponds to each of them) showing agglomerations of data in specific areas. This provides a starting point for the definition of the macro-clusters of an aggregate segmentation strategy.

Aggregate segmentation and segments of one
Lewis *et alia*[7] propose, for the SOM model, to designate as macro-cluster centroids those nodes with the largest number of patterns mapped onto it. Each of the remaining nodes will be added to the macro-cluster with the closest centroid. An example of these methods is the 9-segment solution in *figure 5(a)*. Those segments have to be interpreted in terms of the segmentation bases. Two methods for the interpretation of the segments are described next.

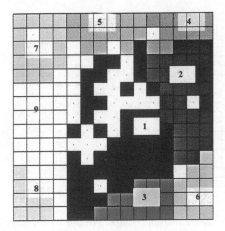

Figure 5: (a) A 9-segment solution obtained with the clustering procedure described in the text. It is interpreted in *table 4* with the help of the *reference maps* in *figure 6* and the *contribution maps* in *figure 7*.

Reference maps

The *reference vectors* $\mathbf{m}_i = \mathbf{W}\phi(\mathbf{u}_i)$ in data space, for each node i in latent space, can be used to describe the segments. Each of the variables shaping these vectors can be visualized using a *reference map*, which is a pseudo-colour representation of its numerical values. The reference maps for our trained GTM are shown in *figure 6*. The meaning of the numerical values (white for high, black for low in a grey-shaded palette) is described in *table 3*.

Contribution of the factors to the segment structure

The influence of each of the factors on the overall cluster / segment structure can further be assessed[28] by measuring the contribution of each reference vector component to the total distance between map units, defined as

$$\left| m_{ik} - m_{jk} \right| / \left\| \mathbf{m}_i - \mathbf{m}_j \right\|, \tag{11}$$

where i and j are two neighbouring units in latent space, and $k = 1,\ldots,5$ for our 5-factor selection. For each unit, these contributions can be averaged over all its neighbours and visualized using a pseudo-colour representation. The resulting

COMPATIBILITY   RISK PERCEPTION   AFFORDABILITY

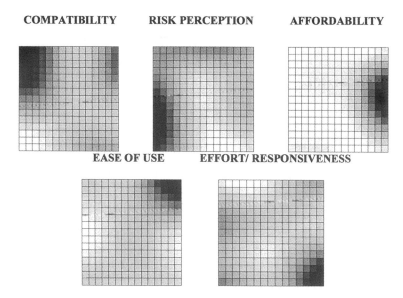

EASE OF USE   EFFORT/ RESPONSIVENESS

Figure 6: Reference maps of the trained GTM, associated with each of the factors in the 5-factor selection, in a pseudo-colour representation. (Light-dark) shades of grey correspond to (high-low) values of the elements of the reference vectors. The interpretation of those high and low values is reported in *table 3.*

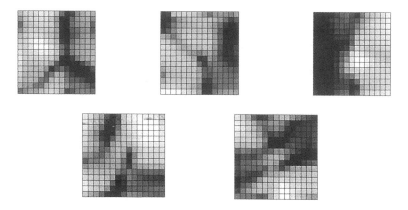

Figure 7: Contribution maps for the trained GTM, describing the influence of each of the factors (in the same order shown in figure 6) on the cluster structure of each region of the map. The numerical values resulting from (11) are visualized in (light-dark) shades of grey correspond to (high-low) values.

	POSITIVE VALUES	NEGATIVE VALUES
Factor 1 *Compatibility*	People who perceive shopping on the WWW as compatible and convenient, feeling they are in control of the shopping process.	People who do not perceive shopping on the WWW as either compatible or convenient, or do not feel in control of the shopping process.
Factor 2 *Risk perception*	People who do not perceive that shop- ping online entails a differential risk. They find online vendors trustworthy.	People who perceive security and economic risks as major deterrents to shop online. They find online vendors untrustworthy.
Factor 3 *Affordability*	People who find the whole prerequisites for online shopping as affordable.	People who find the whole prerequisites for online shopping as unaffordable.
Factor 4 *Ease of use*	People who find shopping online as a complicated undertaking, difficult to learn, that requires a lot of mental effort.	People who find shopping online easy and unproblematic.
Factor 5 *Effort /* *Responsiveness*	People who consider that online vendors provide a responsive customer service, reducing the effort involved in the online shopping process.	People who do not consider that online vendors provide a responsive customer service.

Table 3: Interpretation of the low and high (negative / positive) values of the factor scores (inputs to the model) and reference vectors of the trained GTM.

contribution maps, in *figure 7*, complement the information conveyed by the previously displayed *reference maps*.

It is now possible to use all this information to interpret the suggested 9-segment solution. This interpretation, together with the proposed label and size of the segments, is summarized in *table 4*.

The GTM can also be used to discriminate *segments of one*, a process otherwise referred to as micro-segmentation, one-to-one-segmentation or finer-segmentation[29], by augmenting the latent-space grid to a sufficient resolution. The resulting segments can be characterized using the *reference* and *contribution* maps as described above. Nevertheless, it has to be borne in mind that segments do not naturally arise from the data description of the market, and there is always a degree of subjectivity regarding its definition, motivated by the need to obtain a market description of managerial relevance. At the end of the day, the characteristics of the segments have to be adapted to accommodate a trade off between the costs of the segmentation and the efficiency and likelihood of consumer response[16,30].

SEGMENT DESCRIPTION	LABEL and SIZE (%)
1	*Reference maps:* All factors present medium-to-high values. Values of *Perception of risk, Affordability* and *Effort/Responsiveness* are especially high. *Contribution maps:* medium to high influence of all factors in specific regions of the map.*(91.0% purchasers – 9.0% non-purchasers)*	*Convinced* (22.7%)
2	*Reference maps:* Most factors present medium values except *Affordability*, which is very low. *Contribution maps:* Medium influence of *Affordability* and medium-to-high influence of *Ease of use.(27.7% purchasers – 72.3% non-purchasers)*	*Cost conscious* (16.7%)
3	*Reference maps:* High values of *Affordability* and *Perception of risk*, but rather low values of *Effort/responsiveness*. *Contribution maps:* High influence of *Effort/responsiveness* and medium influence of *Compatibility, Perception of risk* and *Affordability* in specific regions. *(71.2% purchasers – 28.8% non-purchasers)*	*Security and cost confident* (9.4%)
4	*Reference maps*: Low *Compatibility* and very low *Ease of use*. Medium to high *Affordability*. *Contribution maps:* High influence of *Ease of use.(19.6% purchasers – 80.4% non-purchasers)*	*Complexity avoiders* (5.9%)
5	*Reference maps*: Similar to the segment 7 but scoring higher in the factor of *Compatibility*. *Contribution maps:* Medium-to-high influence of all factors, but *Affordability*, in some regions.*(58.7% purchasers – 41.3% non-purchasers)*	*Undecided* (9.6%)
6	*Reference maps*: This small group scores very low in *Effort/responsiveness*, but medium-to-high in the rest of factors. *Contribution maps:* Medium-to-high influence of *Effort/responsiveness* and *Affordability*. *(45.4% purchasers – 54.6% non-purchasers)*	*Customer service wary* (5.6%)
7	*Reference maps*: Very low on *Compatibility* and rather low on *Perception of risk*, although rather high on *Affordability*. *Contribution maps:* Medium influence of *Compatibility, Ease of use* and *Effort/responsiveness.(14.5% purchasers – 85.5% non-purchasers)*	*Unconvinced* (8.9%)
8	*Reference maps*: High *Compatibility* compounded with low values of *Perception of risk*. *Contribution maps:*Medium-to-high influence of *Perception of risk*, and medium influence of *Compatibility* and *Ease of use.(31.7% purchasers – 68.3% non-purchasers)*	*Security conscious* (5.3%)
9	*Reference maps*: High on *Affordability* and *Ease of Use*, but low in all the risk related factors. *Contribution maps:* Medium-to-high influence of *Compatibility*, medium influence of *Perception of risk*, and medium influence of *Ease of use* in some regions *(36.3% purchasers – 63.7% non-purchasers)*	*Risk avoiders* (15.9%)

Table 4: Description of the segments corresponding to the 9-segment solution proposed in the text. They are numbered, according to the labels in *figure 5(a)*, in the first column of the table, and described in the second column according to the *reference maps* and the *contribution maps*. This column also includes the percentages of *purchasers* and *non-purchasers* present in each segment. The relative size of the segments is included in the third column together with their proposed labels.

Outliers detection

The spread of values of the reference vectors can be used for the detection of potential outliers in the original data set[24]. This is because the reference vectors, a product of the mapping, are only expected to cover the areas of higher data occurrence. A comparison of the histograms corresponding to each of the components of both the reference vectors and the original factors should permit visualization of those potential outliers. For our data, the histograms are shown in figure 8.

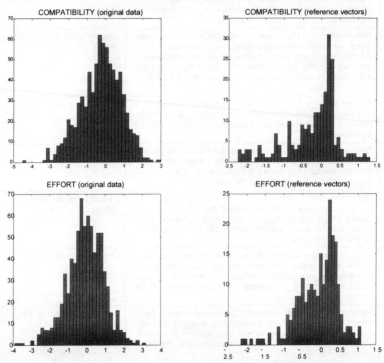

Figure 8: Pairs of histograms representing the spread of values of both the original data (for only two factors, for the sake of brevity) and the corresponding representations learnt by the GTM. Their comparison shows that the mapping generated by the model does not include the extreme values of the original factor scores. This information could be used to single out those individuals in the data set that might be considered outliers.

Fuzzy clustering

The posterior probability of node / segment-membership (5) provides a wealth of information for each consumer that is lost in the representations of the complete set of data. Assuming that each individual belongs only to one cluster (non-overlapping clustering) but the information it conveys does not suffice to uniquely assess the cluster membership[16,31], this information would be the basis for the use of the GTM as a fuzzy clustering tool. According to Wedel and Kamakura[16], the use of fuzzy segmentation techniques "affords a better theoretically founded representation of markets". *Figure 9* displays the posterior probability for a couple of individual cases.

Case 1   **Case 2**

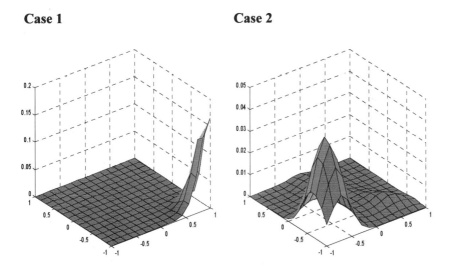

Figure 9: Representation of the posterior probability of node / segment-membership (8) for two specific consumers. This probability adds up to 1 over the 225 nodes of the 15x15 grid. Case 1 clearly corresponds to segment 6 (*Customer service wary*) of the 9-segment solution described in *table 4*. Case 2 belongs to segment 9 (*Risk avoiders*) but it is very close to segment 8 (*Security conscious*) and segment 1 (*Convinced*). Making use of the reference maps, it is clear that this consumer would be much more likely to become a *purchaser* if the perception of risk (factor 2 in *table 1*) was alleviated.

5   Conclusions

The application of exploratory factor analysis has demonstrated the existence of a parsimonious latent structure underlying customers opinions towards online shopping, explainable in meaningful, marketing-operative terms. As a result of the latent variable selection, the importance of *Consumer risk perception / Environmental control* as the main discriminator between the classes of online purchasers and non-purchasers entirely supports the statements in Hoffman et al.[12], pointing to the lack of consumer trust -materialised in "concerns over information privacy in electronic, networked environments"- as the main restraining factor for online shopping adoption. The weak predictive capabilities of demographic, socio-economic and web usage variables, suggest that management decision making could be focused on factors under *in-house* control (*Consumer risk perception, Shopping experience, Customer service, Environmental control*). The satisfactory degree of accuracy to which a very parsimonious description of the original data has been able to predict propensity to buy online reinforces the practical managerial value of using quantitative methods in e-commerce market analysis.

In the context of Internet retailing, the identification of clusters of consumer types has been stated as "the most important use of data mining, as this type of information is useful in a myriad of other planning and development tasks"[3]. The neural network-inspired GTM, a non-linear latent variable model for market segmentation and data visualization with a probabilistic formulation, has been shown to accommodate both one-to-one and traditional aggregate segmentation models. The probabilistic formulation of the GTM also makes possible its use as a fuzzy clustering tool.

This model has been used to analyze data concerning consumers' opinions of online shopping. It has been shown that the GTM can discriminate, to a high degree, the classes of on-line purchasers and non-purchasers *without any a priori information* of the class membership of the individuals in the sample. This reinforces similar results obtained with the SOM model[32]. Examples of the use of the GTM for aggregate segmentation, outlier detection and fuzzy clustering have also been provided.

Factor analysis of the data on Internet users opinions towards online shopping, followed by prediction of propensity to buy online and market segmentation can be seen as the building blocks of a decision support system for online marketers. Neural Networks have been shown to be robust techniques for classification/prediction as well as useful visualization tools for cluster-based market segmentation.

References

1. B.J. Farquhar and A. Balfour. Consumer needs in global electronic commerce: The role of standards in addressing consumer concerns. *EM: Electronic Markets Newsletter*, **8**(2), 1-5.

2. C.M. Bishop, M. Svensén, and C.K.I. Williams. 1998a. GTM: the Generative Topographic Mapping. *Neural Computation* **10**(1), 215-234.

3. D. Slater, M. Mulvenna, A. Büchner, and L. Moussy. 1999. Mining marketing intelligence from Internet retailing data: user requirements & business process description. *Proceedings of the European Multimedia, Microprocessor Systems and Electronic Commerce (EMMSEC'99) Annual Conference.* Stockholm, Sweden.

4. C. Kehoe, J. Pitkow, and J.D. Rogers. 1998. *9th GVU's WWW user survey.* http://www.gvu.gatech.edu/user_surveys/survey-1998-04/

5. D.J. Hand. 1997. *Construction and Assessment of Classification Rules*, (Chichester: John Wiley & Sons)

6. P.E. Green, and A. M. Krieger, A.M. 1995. Alternative approaches to cluster-based market segmentation. *Journal of the Market Reseach Society* **37**(3), 221-239.

7. W.J. Krzanowski. 1996. *Principles of Multivariate Analysis*, (Oxford: Clarendon Press)

8. H.F. Kaiser. 1974. An Index of Factorial Simplicity. *Psychometrica* **39**, 31-36.

9. S.L. Jarvenpaa and P.A. Todd. 1996/97. Consumer reactions to electronic shopping on the WWW. *International Journal of Electronic Commerce*, **1**(2), 59-88.

10. M. Brannback. 1997. Is the Internet changing the dominant logic of marketing? *European Management Journal*, **15**(6), 698-707.

11. D.L. Hoffman and T.P. Novak. 1997. A new marketing paradigm for electronic commerce. *The Information Society*, **13**(1), 43-54.

12. D.L. Hoffman, T.P. Novak, and M.A. Peralta. 1999. Information privacy in the marketspace: implications for the commercial uses of anonymity on the Web. *The Information Society*, **15**(2), 129-139.

13. D.J.C. Mackay. 1995. Probable networks and plausible predictions - a review of practical Bayesian methods for supervised neural networks network-computation in neural systems. *Network: Computation in Neural Systems*, **6**, 469-505.

14. P. Bradley. 1997. The use of the area under the ROC curve in the evaluation of machine learning algorithms. *Pattern Recognition*, **30**(7), 1145-1159.

15. D.J.C. Mackay. 1992. The evidence framework applied to classification networks. *Neural Computation*, **4**(5), 720-736.

16. M. Wedel and W.A. Kamakura. 1998. *Market Segmentation: Conceptual and Methodological Foundations*. (Massachusetts: Kluwer Academic Publishers)

17. C.M. Bishop, M. Svensén, and C.K.I. Williams. 1998a. GTM: the Generative Topographic Mapping. *Neural Computation* **10**(1), 215-234.

18. C.M. Bishop, M. Svensén, and C.K.I. Williams. 1998b. Developments of the Generative Topographic Mapping. *Neurocomputing* **21**(1-3), 203-224

19. T. Kohonen. 1982. Self-organized formation of topologically correct feature maps. *Biological Cybernetics*, **43**(1), 59-69.

20. T. Kohonen. 1995. *Self-Organizing Maps*. (Berlin: Springer-Verlag)

21. G.R. Hinton, C.K.I. Williams, and M.D. Revow. 1992. Adaptive elastic models for hand-printed character recognition. In J.E. Moody, S.J. Hanson, and R.P. Lippmann (Eds.) *Advances in Neural Information Processing Systems*, Vol.4. 512-519. (Morgan Kauffmann)

22. A.P. Dempster, N.M. Laird, and D.B. Rubin. 1977. Maximum likelihood from incomplete data via the EM algorithm. *Journal of the Royal Statistical Society, B*, **39**(1), 1-38.

23. B. Ripley. 1996. *Pattern recognition and neural networks*. (Cambridge University Press)

24. J. Vesanto. 1999. SOM-based data visualization. *Intelligent Data Analysis*, 3(2), 111-126.

25. C.M. Bishop, M. Svensén, and C.K.I. Williams. 1997. Magnification Factors for the GTM Algorithm. In *Proceedings IEE Fifth International Conference on Artificial Neural Networks*, 64-69, Cambridge, U.K.

26. A. Ultsch. 1993. Self-organizing neural networks for visualization and classification. In O. Opitz, B. Lausen, and R. Klar (Eds.), *Information and classification. Concepts, methods and applications*, 307-313. (Berlin: Springer-Verlag)

27. O.M. Lewis, J.A. Ware, and D. Jenkins. 1997. A novel neural network technique for the valuation of residential property. *Neural Computing & Applications* 5(4), 224-229.

28. S. Kaski, J. Nikkilä, and T. Kohonen. 1998. Methods for interpreting a self-organized map in data analysis. In *Proceedings of European Symposium on Artificial Neural Networks (ESANN)*, Bruges, Belgium.

29. A. Kara and E. Kaynak. 1997. Markets of a single customer: exploiting conceptual developments in market segmentation. *European Journal of Marketing*, 31(11-12), 873-895.

30. Y. Wind. 1978. Issues and Advances in Segmentation Research. *Journal of Marketing Research*, 15(August), 317-337.

31. G.J. McLachlan and K.E. Basford. 1988. *Mixture Models: Inference and Applications to Clustering*. (New York: Marcel Dekker)

32. A. Vellido, P.J.G. Lisboa, and K. Meehan. 1999. Segmentation of the on-line shopping market using neural networks. *Expert Systems with Applications*, 17(4), 303-314.

Chapter 4

A Neurofuzzy Model for Predicting Business Bankruptcy

A.H. Boussabaine and M. Wanous
School of Architecture & Building Engineering
The University of Liverpool
Liverpool, L69, 3BX
E-mail: A.H.Boussabaine@liverpool.ac.uk

1   Introduction

The bankruptcy of businesses can be attributed to many factors. Amongst these factors are bad decision making, unforeseen market conditions, economic conditions, lack of knowledge of the market, economic recession, illiquidity, etc. Information about these factors is not apparent to managers, decision-makers, investors, shareholders and creditors. However, this information might easily be extracted from the assessment of several financial ratios, singly and combined, before business failure.

This chapter develops and models business bankruptcy prediction using neurofuzzy modelling techniques. The application might be of assistance to auditors, investors, business managers, bankers and others in making decisions about investments. Developing a robust and reliable model for bankruptcy prediction is important to allow an independent evaluation of the risk of investments.

Every business is considered to be at risk of bankruptcy even if it is expected to continue in existence for the foreseeable future. Investors and business managers must evaluate the risk associated with the ability of a business to continue operating for a reasonable time. If risk and doubt exists about its continued existence, then potential risk factors must be examined and analysed before any investment decision is taken place. Uncertainty and fuzziness of information on financial statements, laws and other information further complicate this process.

This calls for hybrid decision support systems that can learn from the past performance of a business and take into account fuzziness in the assessment of bankruptcy risk. Therefore, the first part of this chapter deals with the theory and principles for modelling business bankruptcy and demonstrates the advantage neurofuzzy modelling techniques bring to the business community. The second section describes the steps and processes involved in developing such models. The third part presents and discusses the results generated by the developed model. The final part evaluates and compares developed models.

2   Methods for modelling business bankruptcy

The task of forecasting business bankruptcy can be posed as a classification problem, given a set of classes and a set of input data instances, each described by a suitable set of features. Each input data instance may be assigned to one of the classes. For this paper, five financial ratios form the set of input data instances and the various business financial performance scenarios (e.g., bankrupt, non- bankrupt etc.) form the set of possible classes to which the input characteristic of each businesses may belong. Each can be described by a set of features, which represent important information about the financial performance of the business.

Let p represent the space of n businesses therefore: $P_1, P_2 \ldots \ldots P_n$, and r be the set of possible (mutually exclusive) m classes of businesses ratings according to their financial performance, $R_1, R_2 \ldots \ldots R_m$. Let f represent the k dimensional feature space $F_1, F_2 \ldots \ldots F_k$ describing each business. Each business can be considered as a k-cluster $F_{1_{Bi}} \ldots \ldots F_{k_{Bi}}$ in the Cartesian space $F_1 \times F_2 \times \ldots \ldots F_k$. Finding the state of a business involves finding the one to one majority function f: $fF_1 \times F_2 \times \ldots \ldots F_x \ldots \ldots R$. The mapping produced by this function f i.e. the bankruptcy of a business, is determined from past experience (from financial ratios) but a precise functional form or a mathematical model of this is not known. This is an approximation to this feature space, which can be defined. There are two possible methods for modelling function f. These are:

2.1   Traditional methods

Traditional linear discriminant functions have been used to analyse financial data for bankruptcy or financial distress analysis. These models are built on many restrictive assumptions. For example, the distribution of discriminating variables is assumed to be jointly multivariate normal. It was found that the results of discriminant analysis procedures is erroneous when the above assumption is violated[1]. Altman[2] has developed a model using multiple discriminant analysis techniques to predict business bankruptcy by combining several financial ratios into a single index. It was found that Altman's models were both novel and highly reliable. However, the model was developed mainly to assess the financial strength of businesses by classifying them into two categories, failing and non-failing business. The statistical methods used were unable to model the overlap (fuzziness) between bankrupt and potentially non-bankrupt classes. Wilcox[3] developed a bankruptcy model based on the inflows and outflows of liquid resources. Dhumale[1] has developed a logit regression model to analyse and predict bankruptcy. This model is conceptually preferred to models such as the linear discriminant model because the assumption of multivariate normality is not required for independent variables[4].

This brief review shows that while there are a number of publications on modelling business bankruptcy, most models are based on statistical techniques whereby the best fit is sought. In many cases the attributes that determine the financial health of a firm are very difficult to quantify and may not lend themselves to curve fitting since the needed representation cannot nicely fit into a quantitative description. Further, it is often not clear which factor business bankruptcy depends on and the degree of effect such factors may have. The relationship between inputs and outputs in those models are very complex since there may be some unknown combined effects. Hence, it is difficult to perform such multi-attribute non-linear mappings by using statistical methods. Also the statistical models lack the ability to learn by themselves, generalise solutions, and adequately respond to highly correlated, incomplete, or previously unknown data. Artificial intelligence offers an approach to modelling that is different from conventional analytic methods.

2.2 Artificial intelligence

In the last decade a great number of publications have been reported on the application of AI to business processes. These applications are developed for a range of business activities. These includes accounting/auditing, finance, marketing distribution, human resources, etc. Literature review shows that many AI applications were developed in the area of finance and in particular in the fields of stock performance of business[5,6]. For example, Altman et al.[7] report on the comparison between ANN and discriminant analysis for corporate distress diagnosis. Wilson and Sharda[8] used ANN for predicting bankruptcy. Serrano-Cinca[9] investigated the use of self-organising neural networks for financial diagnosis. He also examined the use of feed-forward neural networks in the classification of financial information[10]. Others have used ANN and genetic algorithms for bankruptcy prediction[11].

Expert systems, fuzzy logic and artificial neural networks (ANNs) provide powerful tools that can help managers and decision-makers in modelling business bankruptcy. Expert systems are generally good at representing static knowledge and rules of thumb. Fuzzy techniques have the ability to represent the real world, exploit the tolerance for imprecision and uncertainty in data. ANNs have the ability to learn and generalise from examples, to produce meaningful solutions over time to compensate for changing circumstances, to process information rapidly, and to transfer readily between computing systems. A trained ANN system can be tested, and its accuracy can be assured at some level of statistical significance, but the network does not provide any explanation of the problem under investigation. ANN systems have many advantages over traditional methods of modelling in situations where the process to be modelled is complex to the extent that it cannot be explicitly represented in mathematical terms or that explicit formation causes loss of sensitivity due to over-simplification. ANN systems can provide a precise, non-linear correlation between input and output data, but the mechanism underlying that correlation is opaque. The network parameters (i.e., weights, learning rules, transfer functions, topology, etc.) reveal nothing than can rationally be interpreted as a causal explanation of the real world relationship modelled by the trained network. This opacity problem has two effects on ANN technology. Firstly, it reduces confidence in ANN technology. Secondly, it makes the design of ANN systems ad-hoc based.

Another problem with ANN systems is that with nominal or ordinal representation of input and output, useful information could be disregarded. However, combining ANN systems with qualitative causal models can solve this problem of opacity[12]. Combining neural network systems with fuzzy models helps to explain their behaviour and to validate their performance. The most common approach for combining qualitative causal models with ANN systems is the neurofuzzy approach. Neurofuzzy technique is a combination of the explicit knowledge representation of fuzzy logic with the learning power of neural networks. The theory of fuzzy sets provides a suitable method of analysing complex systems and decision processes when the pattern of indeterminacy is due to inherent variability or vagueness rather than randomness[12]. The decision making process of managers is characterised by their capability in handling vague and imprecise concepts that are often expressed linguistically. Fuzzy concepts can help financial managers to make reliable decisions with ambiguous and imprecise events or facts by representing them in linguistic terms. Decision-makers usually assign linguistic values of fuzzy nature to their forecast or description of events. For example, the risk of a business going under may be considered 'possible', 'unlikely', highly-probable, 'certain', and so on. These words are fuzzy sets. They represent the fundamental imprecision that is associated with the formation of concepts. Other advantages of neurofuzzy techniques over other modelling methods include[13, 14]:

- Rules and real world performance data are blended
- Rules and input / output variables are selected and optimised during training
- Non-contributing variables to the decision process are identified and eliminated
- Neurofuzzy models are re-trainable when new data and knowledge become available
- Text and visual reasons for results are provided

3   Data selection

The selection of data and financial attributes that are sensitive in predicting the performance of a firm is a very important step in any model development. Financial attributes that are efficient indicators of financial health and performance of any business must be very sensitive to changes in business internal and external environment and must also be able to correctly measure business handling of unexpected market conditions. The rule of thumb is that the more sensitive a financial attribute is to bankruptcy risk, the more likely it will show changes in the financial health of a business, and therefore, the more effective it will be as a measure for developing early warning systems. This work uses financial ratios that have been proven to be efficient as indicators for predicting the performance of a firm. Five financial ratios were used to develop the model. These ratios are related to financial performance of these firms. These ratios are the same as those employed by previous studies[15]. These are:

1. Working capital/ total assets (WC/TA)
2. Retained earnings/ total assets (RE/TA)
3. Earning before interest and tax/ total assets (EBIT/TA)
4. The market value of equity/total debt (MVE/TD)
5. Sales/total assets (S/TA)

Although several models for forecasting bankruptcy have been developed, the model generated by this work uses data from previous studies, which used statistical and neural network methods. Moreover, this is one of the firsts' studies to use neurofuzzy methods for analysing business bankruptcy. The data are the same as the ones used by (Odom and Sharda[16], and Rahimian et al.[15]). The data sample is divided into two sub-samples. The training sub-sample contained 74 firms, 36 non-bankrupt and 38 bankrupt firms. The testing sample consisted of 55 firms, 28 non-bankrupt and 27 bankrupt firms.

The data of previous studies was used to enable comparison and cross validation of the developed model.

4   Neurofuzzy modelling of business bankruptcy

The process of development of neurofuzzy models is outlined in Fig. 1. The process starts with the evaluation and assessment of the suitability of AI tools to solve the problem under investigation. The criteria for evaluation can be found in Altrock[17].

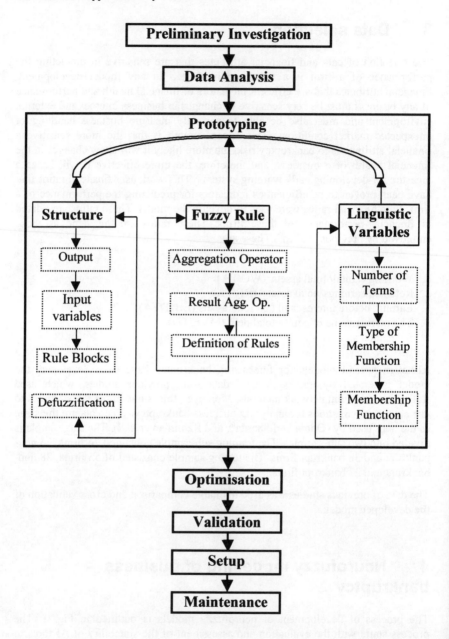

Figure 1: The neurofuzzy modelling process.

Having decided that AI methods are the best for solving your problems, data has to be collected and analysed. The purpose here is to learn more about the nature of the data and the problem under investigation; to solve problems in data; to change the structure of data (levels of granularity); to extract meaningful knowledge and analysis of the qualitative variables and quantitative variables.

The next important stage is prototyping. This involves the definition of input and output variables and the types of decisions that the neurofuzzy system will make. The expected outcome of this stage is the creation of an empty fuzzy logic knowledge base (i.e., rules) ready for training. This system is then trained, optimized, tested, validated and deployed in the real world if the performance is satisfactory.

4.1   Structure of the model

Fig.2 shows the structure of the developed model. The structure consists of input interfaces, rule blocks and output variables. The connecting lines indicate the data flow. The model structure identifies the fuzzy logic inference flow from the input variables to the output variables. The fuzzification in the input interfaces translates financial input ratios into fuzzy values. The fuzzy inference takes place in rule blocks, which contain the linguistic control rules. The output of these rule blocks is linguistic variables. The defuzzification in the output interfaces translates them into bankrupt non-bankrupt classes.

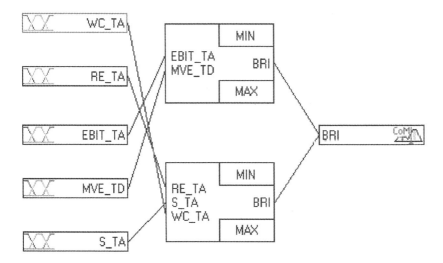

Figure 2: Structure of the bankruptcy neurofuzzy model

Five input variables were selected based on past studies and their ability to detect business financial distress. The real values of the input and output variables are translated into linguistic values. The possible values of a linguistic variable are not numbers but so called 'linguistic terms'. For example; to translate the real variable 'Working capital/ total assets (WC_TA)' into a linguistic variable three terms, 'low, 'medium' and 'high' are defined. Depending on the financial health of a business each of these terms describes this financial ratio more or less well. Each term is defined by a membership function (MBF). Each membership function defines for any value of the input variable, the associated degree of membership of the linguistic term. Membership function definitions should obey the following conditions[17]:

1. $\mu(x)$ continuous over X, small change in the input variables must not result in a step in its evaluation
2. $\mu'(x)$ continuous over X, small change in the input variables must not result in a step in its evaluation rate
3. $\mu''(x)$ continuous over X, this is necessary for satisfying the next condition
4. μ: $\min_\mu\{\max_x\{\mu''(x)\}\}$ for all X, the change in slope should be minimal

Cubic interpolative S shaped function satisfies these conditions. Therefore, a S shaped function was used for input and output variables. Fig. 3 (See Appendix) shows the membership functions and linguistic terms of the variables used in the bankruptcy model. Table 1 lists all linguistic variables of the model and their term names. The properties of the five input variables are shown in Table 2.

The rule blocks and the interface connections are developed heuristically. In total 22 models were experimented with. The one with the lowest testing error was selected for comparison with the findings from previous studies. Table 5 shows a summary of the optimisation process of the bankruptcy models.

Variable Name	Term Names
EBIT_TA	low, medium, high
MVE_TD	low, medium, high
RE_TA	low, medium, high
S_TA	low, medium, high
WC_TA	low, medium, high
BRI	BR_Very_high, BR_High, BR_Medium, BR_Low, BR_Very_Low

Table 1: Input and output variables

Variable Name	Min	Max	Default	Unit
EBIT_TA	-0.4861	0.2994	-0.09335	EBIT_TA
MVE_TD	0.0417	30.6486	15.3452	NVE_TD
RE_TA	-1.6945	0.697	-0.49875	RE_TA
S_TA	0.2216	6.5145	3.36805	S_TA
WC_TA	-0.5359	0.6674	0.06575	WC_TA
BRI	-1.6	1.6	0	BRI

Table 2: Properties of the model variables

The rule blocks contain the control strategy of the fuzzy logic bankruptcy model. Each rule block confines all rules for the same context. A context is defined by the same input and output variables of the rules. These rules are extracted automatically from the training data set. These rules were then trained to identify the strength of any pattern within the data set. Rule block 1 contains 14 rules and has two input variables. Rule bock 2 includes 11 rules and has three input variables. Tables 3 and 4 show the extracted and trained rules. The 'if' part of the rule describes the financial situation of business under assessment for bankruptcy, for which the rules are designed. The 'then' part describes the classification of the business by the fuzzy model. The degree of support (DoS) is used to weigh each rule according to its importance. The DoS values were randomized before training the model. During the training DoS values change according to the pattern in the training data set. The methodology and mathematical background for processing the rules are described in detail in Altrock (1996).

The optimum model was tested with both training and testing data sub-samples. Only three cases from the training data were misclassified, whereas 8 cases from the testing sub-sample were misclassified. The models produced negative indices for three non-bankruptcy cases from the training sub-sample. The average Bankruptcy Indices (BRI) of these cases was (-0.3862). The models did not produce positive indices for any bankruptcy cases. Thus, these findings were used to develop a Confidence Degree (CD) based on the output fiom the model. Fig. 4 shows the confidence degree based on the BRI output from the neurofuzzy model. Fig. 4 indicates that if BRI is above 0 then a business is liquid, whereas a BRI less than (-0.3862) indicates that a business is bankrupt with a very high degree of confidence. But, if the BRI is between (-0.3862 and 0) a business is considered bankrupt with a degree of confidence varying from very high at (-0.3862) to very low when BRI = 0.

IF		THEN	
EBIT_TA	MVE_TD	DoS	BRI
low	low	1.00	BR_Very_high
low	low	0.01	BR_Medium
low	low	0.18	BR_Very_Low
medium	low	0.14	BR_Very_high
medium	low	0.01	BR_Medium
medium	low	0.02	BR_Very_Low
medium	high	0.01	BR_Very_Low
high	low	0.03	BR_High
high	low	0.18	BR_Very_Low
high	medium	0.01	BR_High
high	medium	0.10	BR_Low
high	medium	0.27	BR_Very_Low
high	high	0.05	BR_Medium
high	high	0.45	BR_Very_Low

Table 3: Rules of the Rule Block "RB1"

IF			THEN	
RE_TA	S_TA	WC_TA	DoS	BRI
low	low	low	0.14	BR_Very_Low
low	low	medium	0.03	BR_Low
low	low	high	0.99	BR_High
medium	low	low	0.02	BR_Medium
medium	low	medium	1.00	BR_Very_high
medium	low	high	0.98	BR_Very_high
medium	low	high	1.00	BR_High
high	low	low	0.02	BR_Very_Low
high	low	high	0.01	BR_Very_high
high	low	high	0.02	BR_Very_Low
high	medium	high	0.11	BR_High

Table 4: Rules of the Rule Block "RB2"

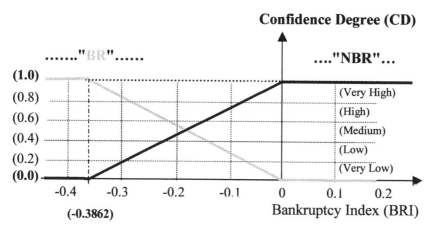

Figure 4: The confidence degree based on the BRP index

Therefore the following rules might be used to compute a confidence degree for each forecast from the neurofuzzy model.

If BRI < -0.3862 then $CD_{br} = 1$;

If -0.382 < BRI < 0 $CD_{br} = (0.3862+BRI)/ 0.3862$;

If BRI > 0 then $CD_{br} = 0$; and,

$CD_{nbr} = 1 - CD_{br.}$

Where:
BRI: Bankruptcy Index;
CD_{br}: Confidence Degree in bankruptcy; and,
CD_{nbr}: Confidence degree in non-bankruptcy.

5 Results and discussion

The results of test runs on the 22 models are included Table 5. The best performance was achieved by model 18 with an accuracy of 47/55 cases. The training and testing results reflect the behaviour of the extracted fuzzy knowledge base from the training data. The results showed a modest improvement on previous studies. Also this model has the advantage of transparency and explanation of the importance of the financial ratios contribution to business failure provided by the if-then rules. Model 18 included two rule blocks and five financial ratios. Failed businesses were assigned a BRI index of 0, whereas liquid firms were assigned a BRI of 1. Hence, a negative prediction suggested that a business is in financial

Model	Inputs		Rule Blocks			Outputs			Learning		Testing	
	No.	Terms No.	Shape	No.	Operator Type	Parameter	No.	Terms No.	Shape	Av. Dev.	Iteration	Av. Dev.	Mis-class.
1	5	3	S	2	Min	0			S	22.99	62	28.92	15
2	5	3	S	2	Min	0			S	19.78	32	27.83	13
3	5	3	S	2	Min	0			S	17.90	21	25.10	13
4	5	3	L	2	Min	0			L	19.27	25	27.09	16
5	5	3	L	2	Min	0			L	10.26	48	19.81	13
6	5	3	L	2	Min	0			L	19.19	26	27.16	18
7	5	3	L	2	?	0.10			L	10.66	41	19.70	13
8	5	5	L	2	?	0.10			L	19.76	32	27.93	16
9	5	5	S	2	?	0.10			L	19.47	21	27.92	17
10	5	3	S	2	Min	0			S	17.44	21	27.20	19
11	3	3	L	1	?	0.10			S	18.34	15	27.97	15
12	5	3	S	2	?	0.10	1	5	S	20.36	24	27.45	14
13	5	3	L	2	Min	0			L	9.83	15	18.38	14
14	5	3	L	2	Min	0			L	9.83	16	17.06	13
15	5	3	S	2	Min	0			S	9.69	12	17.96	13
16	5	3	S	2	Min	0			S	8.31	23	18.51	13
17	5	3	S	2	Min	0			S	9.32	26	17.68	11
18	5	3	S	2	Min	0			S	**9.73**	34	**16.50**	**8**
19	5	3	S	2	Min	0			S	9.54	45	16.53	11
20	5	3	S	2	Min	0			S	9.49	61	16.23	9
21	5	3	S	2	Min	0			S	8.91	64	15.66	12
22	5	3	S	2	Min	0			S	8.76	78	16.61	11

Table 5: Optimisation of the developed models.

difficulty, whereas a positive prediction suggests that the risk of bankruptcy is reduced.

Figures 5-11 (See appendix) show results of the generated fuzzy knowledge base. Fig. 5 shows that a firm is classified as bankrupt if it had a lower EBIT/TA and MVE/TD ratio, whereas a business is classified as borderline, if it had a higher MVT/TD and lower EBIT/TA ratio. A firm is considered healthy if it had a high EBIT/TA and MVE/TD ratio. Fig. 6 demonstrates that if EBIT/TA and RE/TA ratios are both negative and low the chances for bankruptcy increases, whereas if RE/TA and EBIT/TA ratios are both positive and very high the chances for bankruptcy are very low. Fig. 7 shows that if S/TA is very high and RE/TA has any value then a business should remain more liquid that their counterparts with medium to very low S/TA. Businesses with a very high RE/TA ratio and a high or medium, or low S/TA ratio are financially healthy. The figure also shows those businesses with a medium RE/TA and medium to low S/TA ratio are at risk of bankruptcy. Fig. 8 demonstrates that whatever the MVE/TD and S/TA ratios are, whether, low, medium, or high, the risk for bankruptcy is always very low. Fig. 9 shows the effect of the variables WC/TA and S/TA on business bankruptcy outcome. The curve can be interpreted as follows: for S/TA = high or low and whatever the WC/TA ratio the BRI index is high and the chances of a firm going bankrupt is very low. However, if the S/TA is medium and WC/TA is high BRI is medium and the business is borderline for bankruptcy. Fig. 10 illustrates the effect of EBIT/TA and S/TA ratios on business bankruptcy. The figure indicates that for high EBIT/TA ratios and whatever the value of S/TA a business remains liquid. However, for a medium to very low EBIT/TA ratio the chance of bankruptcy increases dramatically. Fig. 11 shows that WC/TA and EBIT/TA ratios have similar effects on the prediction of business bankruptcy as in Fig. 10.

The above results show that some of the financial ratios are strongly associated with business failure prediction, whereas others are associated with non-bankruptcy. These results are supportive of situations in which decision makers are charged with avoiding potentially troublesome investment whilst increasing business by taking on perhaps risky but otherwise healthy investment in firms.

5.1 Evaluation

By using the same data as previous studies it was possible to compare the performance of the neurofuzzy method with other modelling techniques. The results of this comparison are presented in Table 6. This table shows the classification results of the various modelling methods. The neurofuzzy method compares favourably with other models, especially model 18 which uses 5 financial ratios carries an 85% accuracy. This modest improvement in performance could be attribute to the fact that the data used in the model has a certain degree of imprecision and fuzziness and the neurofuzzy model was able to map out this behavioural pattern in data.

Model	Modelling Method	Bankruptcy Cases	Non-Bankr. Cases	Overall %
Odom & Sharda	DAT	16	25	74.45
	Backprop.	22	23	81.82
Rahimian, E., et al	Athena	21	24	81.82
	Perceptron	21	24	81.82
	Backprop.	21	24	81.82
Boussabaine et al	NeuroFuzzy	24	23	85.45

Table 6: Comparison of different models. Last column: overall percentage of correct classification.

Another possible explanation of this increase in accuracy could be due to the fact that financial ratios, instability and fuzzy models do not rely on the discovery of strong empirical regularities in observation of the financial performance of business. This is because regularities are not always evident, and are often masked by noise. Also the output from fuzzy models can be easily explained and visualised as demonstrated in the above section.

6   Conclusion

Neurofuzzy systems offer several advantages over traditional methods for the modelling of business bankruptcy. This paper presents an investigation into the prediction of business bankruptcy using a novel analytical technique. Neurofuzzy network predictors may assist managers, decision-makers, investors, shareholders and creditors to make more informed decisions and independently evaluate the risk of investment in businesses

References

1. R. Dhumale. 1998. Earnings retention as a specific mechanism in logistic bankruptcy models: A test of the free cash flow theory. *Journal of Business Finance and Accounting*, **25**(7&8), 1005-1024.

2. E.I. Altman. 1968. Financial ratios, discriminant analysis and the prediction of corporate bankruptcy. *Journal of Finance*, **23**(4), 589-609.

3. J. Wilcox. 1976. The gambler's ruin approach to business risk. *Sloane Management Review*, 33-46.

4. F.M. Richardson and L.F. Davidson. 1983. An exploration into bankruptcy discriminant model sensitivity. *Journal of Business Finance and Accounting*, **10**(2), 195-207.

5. B.K. Wong, T.A. Bodnovich, and Y. Selvi. 1997. Neural network applications in business: A review and analysis of the literature (1988-95). *Decision Support Systems*, **19**, 301-320.

6. A. Vellido, P.J.G. Lisboa, and J. Vaughan. 1999. Neural networks in business: a survey of applications (1992-1998). *Expert Systems with Applications*, **17**(1), 51-70.

7. E.I. Altman, G. Marco, and F. Varetto. 1994. Corporate distress diagnosis: Comparisons using linear discriminant analysis and neural networks. *Journal of Banking and Finance*, **18**, 505-529.

8. R.L. Wilson and R. Sharda. 1994. Bankruptcy prediction using neural networks. *Decision Support Systems*, **11**, 545-557.

9. C. Serrano-Cinca. 1996. Self organizing neural networks for financial diagnosis. *Decision Support Systems.* **17**, 227-238.

10. C. Serrano-Cinca. 1997. Feedforward neural networks in the classification of financial information. *The European Journal of Finance*, **3**(3), 183-202.

11. B. Back, T. Laitinen, and K. Sere. 1996. Neural networks and genetic algorithms for bankruptcy predictions. *Expert Systems with Applications*, **11**(4), 407-413.

12. L.A. Zadeh. 1994. Fuzzy logic, neural networks, and soft computing. *Communication of the ACM*, **37**(3), 77-84.

13. A.H. Boussabaine and T. Elhag. 1998. A fuzzy approach for cash flow analysis. In *Proceedings of the 6ᵗʰ European Congress on Intelligent Techniques & Soft Computing*, Aachen, Germany, Vol. 3, 1975-1984.

14. R. Abbott. 1998. Credit risk rules derived from neurofuzzy data modelling. In *UNICOM, Proceedings on Fuzzy Logic and Soft Computing in Commerce*, 105-128.

15. E. Rahimian, S. Singh, T. Thammachote, and R. Virmani. 1992. Bankruptcy prediction by neural network. In *Neural Networks in Finance and Investment: Using artificial intelligence to improve real world performance*, Edited by R. Trippi and E. Turbain, 159-175.

16. M. Odom and R. Sharda. 1990. A neural network for bankruptcy prediction. *International Joint Conference on Neural Networks*, San Diego, Vol. II, 163-168.

17. C. von Altrock. 1996. *Fuzzy logic and neurofuzzy application in business and finance*. (New Jersey: Prentice Hall).

Appendix

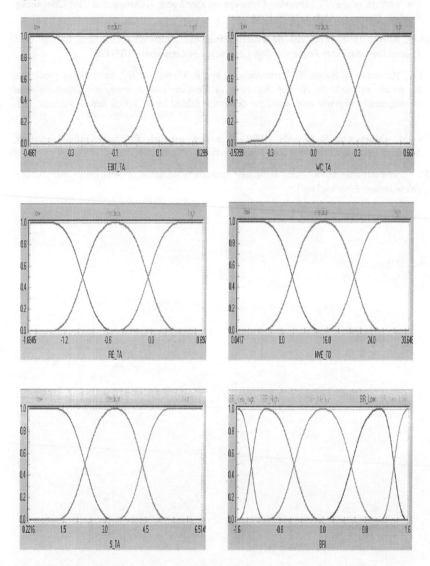

Figure 3: Membership functions of the financial ratios used in the development of the model: Top row: *"EBIT_TA"* (left) and *"WC_TA"* (right). Middle row: *"RE_TA"* (l) and *"MVE_TD"* (r). Bottom row: *"S_TA"* (l) and *"BRI"* (r).

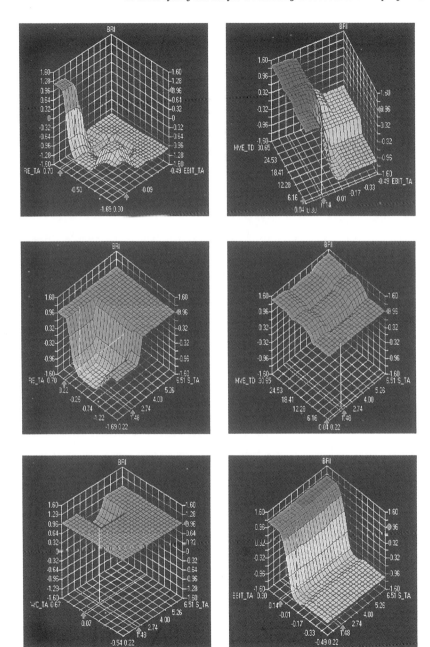

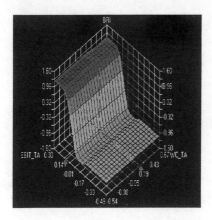

Figures 5-11: Top row to bottom row, left to right: *5*: Relationship between RE/TA, EBIT/TA and BRI. *6*: between MVE/TA, EBIT/TA and BRI. *7*: between RE/TA, S/TA and BRI. *8*: MVE/TA, S/TA and BRI. *9*: between WC/TA, S/TA and BRI. *10*: between S/TA, EBIT/TA and BRI. *11*: between WC/TA, EBIT/TA and BRI.

Chapter 5

Neural Networks for Analysis of Financial Statements

Kimmo Kiviluoto
Laboratory of Computer and Information Science
Helsinki University of Technology
P.O.Box 5400, FIN-02015 HUT, FINLAND
E-mail: kimmo.kiviluoto@hut.fi

Pentti Bergius
Finnvera Ltd.
P.O. Box 1010, FIN-00101 Helsinki, FINLAND
E-mail: pentti.bergius@finnvera.fi

Jyrki Maaranen
Finnvera Ltd.
P.O. Box 1010, FIN-00101 Helsinki, FINLAND
E-mail: jyrki.maaranen@finnvera.fi

1   Introduction

In this chapter, we propose a methodology for analyzing financial statements of an enterprise. The main theme is to show how to transform the numerical data into visual form; the visualization method that we utilize here is based on the Self Organizing Map. We argue that it is often necessary to use three-dimensional map grids instead of the traditional two-dimensional ones, in order to avoid false impressions of the data. We also discuss how to analyze the corporate dynamics based on the trajectories on the map.

The classical methods of financial statement analysis have been based on comparing the financial indicators to some reference values, maybe after first deriving some new indicator from those obtained directly from the financial statements, as is done with the Z-analysis of Altman[1]. These methods describe the

73

state of an enterprise using a collection of numbers. In this section, we propose a method to supplement this classical approach by describing the state of a company using a visual display; as a visualization method, we utilize the Self-Organizing Map (SOM). We start by describing the basics of the SOM, then propose some novel techniques to improve the visualization, and conclude the section by discussing the advantages of visualization of the data and contrasting the SOM to other visualization methods.

2   Mapping the financial statements onto a Self-Organizing Map

The SOM is a neural network algorithm that is widely used to display the relevant information of complex phenomena, hidden into high-dimensional data sets, on a low-dimensional output space. The SOM maps the high-dimensional data onto a low-dimensional map grid in such a manner that the relative distances among the data vectors are approximately preserved.

In the present application, we start by forming a data vector for each financial statement to be analyzed from a few commonly used financial indicators. Then, we train a SOM using the whole set of data vectors, after which we position each data vector (or financial statement) onto the map. Now, we have a map in which similar financial statements are mapped near each other, and the less similar a pair of financial statements is, the greater the distance on the map between the pair. This kind of map can then be used to illustrate the distribution of just about any kind of attribute of the interest, such as the proportion of bankruptcies, degree of growth or profitability, etc.

2.1   The Self-Organizing Map – short introduction

The mapping of the SOM is probably easiest to understand with the aid of Figure 1. Each map unit is linked to some point in the data space: a map unit is associated with a prototype (or weight) vector that contains the data space coordinates the unit is linked to. Then, each data vector – or any point in the data space – can be mapped to the SOM grid by first finding the prototype vector that is closest to the data vector, and then mapping the data vector to the corresponding map unit (BMU, "Best-Matching Unit").

In the training phase of the SOM, the prototype vectors are ordered so that the mapping from data space onto the map becomes approximately smooth, and the prototype vectors also find such locations that they represent well the distribution of the data vectors.

For a more formal discussion of the SOM in the context of the present application, see e.g. Kiviluoto and Bergius[2] and Kiviluoto[3]; for a comprehensive discussion of the SOM in general, an invaluable reference is Kohonen[4].

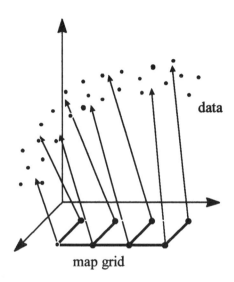

data

map grid

Figure 1: The SOM mapping from a high-dimensional data space onto a low-dimensional map grid.

2.2 Data preparation

The data we have used here consists of the financial statements of the customer companies of Finnvera Ltd, a Finnish risk financing company. From the base population, we excluded those financial statements that were given by very small or startup companies. In the final sample, there were 30 593 financial statements given by 7 028 companies, of which 1 244 eventually failed.

The financial indicators were first chosen using the expert opinion of skilled financial analysts, and they included growth indicators and indicators measuring profitability and solidity. Several different combinations of these indicators were tried, aiming at the best possible separation between healthy enterprises and those that have a high risk of bankruptcy.

As a data preprocessing method, we used componentwise histogram equalization, which for each financial indicator transforms its original, rather highly kurtotic (supergaussian) distribution closer to uniform distribution. Because the original data was already discretized, we did not arrive at exactly uniform distribution, however. The details of how the histogram equalization was performed can be found in the documentation of the SOM Toolbox function `som_normalize_data`[5], using which the preprocessing was performed. The results were qualitatively rather similar when we used variance normalization for data preprocessing, but the classification accuracy was slightly better with histogram equalization.

2.3   Training the map and viewing the results

The SOM was trained with the software packages SOM Toolbox[5] and SOM_PAK[6]. We used linear initialization, and the map training was carried out in one phase of 600 000 learning steps, starting with learning rate value 0.1 and neighborhood radius 3. The bankruptcy indicator was not used in the BMU search, but was updated just like the other components ("Semi-Supervised SOM," see Kiviluoto and Bergius[2]).

We experimented with both two- and three-dimensional SOM's, and as discussed in the next section, found the three-dimensional map better. To visualize the 3D SOM, we needed to slightly modify the SOM Toolbox. An example of a trained map is depicted in Figure 2.

3   Do not oversimplify: 3D SOM's are sometimes better than 2D

The SOM, and many other popular neural network algorithms as well, are well suited to analyze high-dimensional data. However, these algorithms are often based on the implicit assumption that the data is not actually as high-dimensional as it first appears, but that it has interdependencies that allow only certain combinations of the input vector components. Thus, the data does not fill the whole input space but only some subspace or manifold withing the input space. For instance, we might have ten-dimensional input vectors, but a good model might be able to explain all the relevant information that is hidden in the data by using just two variables. Then, the data must live in a two-dimensional subspace of the ten-dimensional input space: the data has an *intrinsic dimension* of two. When the model dimension is lower than the intrinsic dimension of the data, the model must make some tradeoffs. The SOM, for instance, tries to fill the data manifold by folding itself in a manner that is analogous to a one-dimensional Peano curve filling the two-dimensional unit square. This phenomenon has been dubbed "the automatic selection of feature dimensions" by Kohonen[4], and has been rigorously analyzed by Ritter and Schulten[7]. As a result of this folding, the resolution of the mapping from the data manifold onto the SOM lattice improves, but only at the cost of introducing discontinuities in the mapping[8].

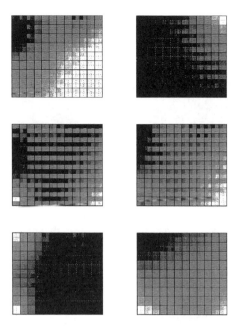

Figure 2: An example of different views to the same SOM – the SOM is here first colored with the relative bankruptcy frequencies and then with the five different financial indicators that determine the location of each financial statement on the SOM. On the top left panel is shown the bankruptcy frequency; dark shade corresponds to high proportion of bankruptcies. On top right, the growth is depicted: note how financial statements given by high-growth companies get mapped into a single cluster on the top right corner of the SOM. On the middle row, two indicators that measure the profitability. On the bottom left, an indicator measuring the indebtness, and on the right, an indicator measuring the solidity.

One can reduce the effects of folding by using a stiffer map (larger value for the neighborhood parameter), but this leads to a decrease in map resolution. The SOM thus makes a tradeoff between resolution and continuity of the mapping.

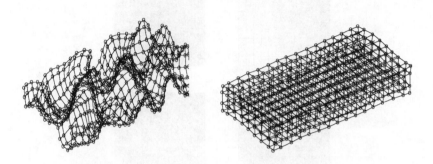

Figure 3: Two- and three dimensional SOM trained with data from a three-dimensional box, shown *in the data space*. The two-dimensional map tries to represent also the third dimension of the data by folding.

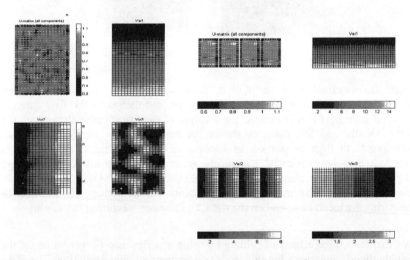

Figure 4: The same maps as in Figure 3, but now shown *in the map space*, as usual – the data space view of Figure 3 becomes impossible when the geometric dimension of the data is more than three. Note how the folds of the two-dimensional SOM (on the left) show erroneously as artefacts especially on the bottom right panel – this extra structure is caused by the incorrect model dimension.

 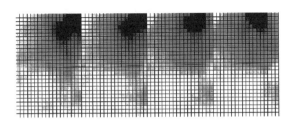

Figure 5: Real-life example of effect of the map dimensionality. On the left, the two-dimensional SOM hints that there are two separate clusters of high bankruptcy risk. On the right, the three-dimensional SOM gives a better approximation, showing that there is only a single "bankruptcy cluster."

In the ideal situation, the dimension of the SOM would thus coincide with the intrinsic dimension of the data. There are certain limitations on increasing the SOM dimensionality, though: the border effect of the SOM[4] grows with the map dimensionality, and visualization of maps with dimensionality higher than three is problematic. However, sometimes already increasing the dimensionality from two to three may improve the results significantly, as shown in Figure 3 and Figure 4 with artificial data and in Figure 5 with real-world data[9].

One of the main problems with 3D-maps is, how to display them so that they are intuitively most understandable? In Figure 6 we have shown the following three alternatives, each with their own strengths and weaknesses:

"Slices" – the map slices are shown blown apart in a 3D-view. Good to demonstrate the overall structure of the map, but less suitable for subsequent more detailed analysis; suffers from the same disadvantages as the 3D graph or bar charts of a standard spreadsheet program, and exaggerates the distances along the third dimension.

"Cards" – the map slices are shown like a hand of playing cards on a table. This is a good display style for viewing each "card" or slice separately, but nearness of neighboring units along the third dimension, i.e. across the slices, is difficult to understand.

"Tartan" – the map slices are squashed together, and units that differ only on their third coordinate are shown next to each other. This is probably the best way to display a 3D map on 2D, when the size of the SOM along the third dimension is small – the impression of distances is close to correct, but still it is possible to observe the changes that occur when moving along the third dimension. However, it takes a little practice to get accustomed to this display style.

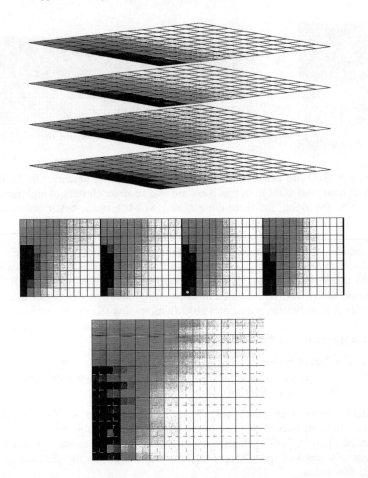

Figure 6: Three possible ways to display the same 3D-SOM: "slices", "cards", "tartan."

Often the most significant structures in the data are well represented in the first two dimensions, which are analogous to the first two principal components in the standard principal component analysis. The "tartan" display style captures this type of structures well. "Cards" display style can then be used to complement the picture, as it shows clearly the differences along the third dimension, between the slices.

Using an interactive display, there are much richer possibilities to visualize 3D SOM's. However, these are currently under research, and the present implementations do not yet seem to add much value to the visualizations on 2D discussed above.

4 Trajectories reveal the dynamics

Above, we have outlined a way to map financial statements from any particular company at any given year onto a SOM. A natural next step is to visualize how the state of a company evolves with time by displaying its *trajectory*, a graph connecting the units the company has been mapped to. Some examples of these corporate trajectories are displayed on Figure 7.

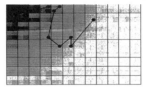

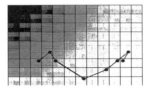

Figure 7: Examples of corporate trajectories. The trajectory on the top, which leads to the bankruptcy region of the map, corresponds to an enterprise that eventually went bankrupt; on the right, a "healthy" trajectory, which ends on the high-profitability, high-solidity region, corresponds to a very succesfull enterprise.

In addition to viewing trajectories of single companies, it is also possible to analyze the typical dynamics withing the training data. In Figure 8, the most typical direction of the next step is shown. One can extend this approach to cover several time steps, perhaps using a second layer SOM, as has been done in Kiviluoto and Bergius[2]. An additional advantage is that this type of model captures well the typical dynamics present in the training data, making it easy to detect anomalies that could be a sign of, for instance, creative accounting, and perhaps worth a closer look.

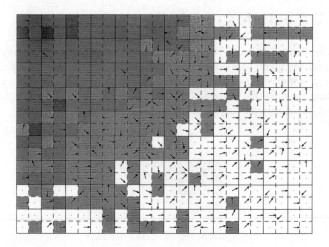

Figure 8: For each map unit, the directions of the most typical next steps are shown. If there is no arrow, the most typical next step is a step to the same unit.

6   Why visualize, and why use SOM's?

Above, we have presented a method for visualizing financial statements, which aims at representing the state of an enterprise with the aid of a single picture. We argue that it is much much easier and faster to absorb information in a visual rather than numeric form. In our application, each region on the SOM has its own characteristics, and one can learn these in a matter hours – much faster than one could get familiar with the different types combinations of numbers typically found in financial statements. In addition, after seeing where a particular enterprise gets mapped to, one instantly has some idea of the shape of that enterprise, whereas even an experienced analyst would need some time to glance through the mass of different financial indicators derived from the financial statements.

Still, visualizing the data with a SOM does not simplify the data too much. It may be argued that bankruptcy models giving only a single figure as an output – Altman's Z-analysis and the like – do give a reasonable bankruptcy estimate, but nothing more. They do not say anything about the type of bankruptcy risks the enterprise is exposed to, or about the dynamics of the enterprise development. In contrast, with the SOM it is easy to, for instance, discriminate between the situations where a company is first suffering from a decrease in profits, and consequently next year has a lower solidity while the profits are already recovering, even though the bankruptcy risk estimate would be the same for both years. This kind of dynamics is especially easy to detect when the SOM is used to analyze the trajectories.

From a more technical point of view, we emphasize using a 3D SOM if the intrinsic dimension of data seems to be more than two. This reduces the risk of introducing artefacts that are not actually present in the data but are caused by the too low dimensionality of the model; as an example, the data may appear to have extra clusters or excessive structure.

Comparing to other visualization methods such as multidimensional scaling (MDS) or Sammon's mapping, the SOM has at least two advantages. It is fast also for large datasets, and it is directly amenable to accommodate new data. We note that the other visualization methods could be modified to overcome these problems by first clustering the data with, say, the k-means algorithm, and then running the visualization algorithm, perhaps with a suitable smoothing that would correspond to the neighborhood function of the SOM. However, essentially this means making them so much like SOM that there hardly is any difference, so one might as well use SOM directly.

References

1. E. I. Altman. 1968. Financial ratios, discriminant analysis, and the prediction of corporate bankruptcy. *The Journal of Finance*, **4**, 589–609.

2. K. Kiviluoto and P. Bergius. 1998. Exploring corporate bankruptcy with two-level self-organizing maps. In *Proceedings of the Fifth International Conference on Computational Finance*, 373–380. (London Business School: Kluwer Academic Publishers).

3. K. Kiviluoto. 1998. Predicting bankruptcies with the self-organizing map. *Neurocomputing*, **21**, 191–201.

4. T. Kohonen. 1995. *Self-Organizing Maps*. Springer Series in Information Sciences 30, (Berlin Heidelberg New York: Springer).

5. E. Alhoniemi, J. Himberg, K. Kiviluoto, J. Parviainen, J. Vesanto. 1997. *SOM Toolbox*. URL http://www.cis.hut.fi/projects/somtoolbox/

6. T. Kohonen, J. Hynninen, J. Kangas, and J. Laaksonen. 1996. *SOM_PAK: The Self-Organizing Map Program Package*. Technical Report A31, Helsinki University of Technology, Laboratory of Computer and Information Science, FIN-02150 Espoo, Finland. URL http://www.cis.hut.fi/nnrc/som_pak/

7. H. Ritter and K. Schulten. "Convergence properties of Kohonen's topology conserving maps: Fluctuations, stability, and dimension selection," Biological Cybernetics, vol. 60(1), pp. 59–71, Nov. 1988.

8. K. Kiviluoto, "Topology preservation in self-organizing maps," in Proceedings of the International Conference on Neural Networks (ICNN'96), vol. 1, (Piscataway, New Jersey, USA), pp. 294–299, IEEE Neural Networks Council, June 1996.

9. K. Kiviluoto. 1998. Comparing 2D and 3D self-organizing maps in financial data visualization. In *Methodologies for the Conception, Design and Application of Soft Computing – Proceedings of the 5th International Conference on Soft Computing and Information/Intelligent Systems (IIZUKA '98)*. Edited by T. Yamakawa and G. Matsumoto. (Singapore: World Scientific), Vol.1, 68–71.

Chapter 6

Developments in Accurate Consumer Risk Assessment Technology

Mark Somers and Greg Piper
Equifax, Decision Solutions, 25 Chapel St., London NW1 5DS UK
E-mail: Mark.Somers@equifax.com

1   Introduction

Assessing the risks inherent in agreeing to grant credit to individuals is at the core of making profitable lending decisions. During the last forty years, driven by computer technology and ever-larger markets, the risk assessment process has become increasingly automated. Scorecards are now the standard technique and are used not only to assess risk but also in a wide variety of other situations, from list selections for customer recruitment, right through to prioritising collections. This report will examine recent work within Equifax, to help in the construction and application of robust, powerful scorecards. Central to the research philosophy has been the desire to examine a wide range of modelling techniques from areas such as Artificial Intelligence, Statistics and Machine Learning. Where these models have been found to be significantly more powerful than the standard techniques, it is sometimes possible to find out why and then to build this extra power into a traditional scorecard.

Recent credit risk conferences and reports have often cited the advances in Artificial Neural Networks as providing a powerful new alternative to traditional scorecards. Despite this the number of neural scorecards actually in operation is still only at a tiny fraction of their overall potential. To understand why, we need to review what is required of a credit-scoring instrument. Of primary concern is that the model constructed must be highly predictive, and it is chiefly on this front that proponents of Neural Networks base their sweeping claims. Equally important however is that the model should be relatively easy to build and redevelop, provide some insight into the factors that influence its operation, be easily compared with current methods (scorecards) and finally be easily implemented on current systems. It is largely the failure of Neural Networks to fulfil these latter requirements (to varying degrees) that has hindered their adoption into the mainstream. To alleviate these problems our research has examined a selection of techniques which can use Neural Network architectures, to build powerful models and then exploit those models to guide the construction of equally powerful scorecards.

2   Optimising scorecard technology

Before detailing the methodology it is worth re-stating why traditional scorecards will under-perform Neural Networks in certain circumstances. The diagram in figure 1 shows a trivial example; in this data set there are two characteristics, age and marital status. Individual cases may be plotted and their good/bad status illustrated by the depth of the shading within the circles. Light shading represents good risks. It is clear from the distribution that there is a strong "reversal" within the data. A scorecard (without interaction terms) would therefore fail to model this data accurately. The background shading in the diagram represents a possible scorecard model. Due to its parametric form a scorecard can only model monotonic changes in predicted risk. A Neural Network by contrast can model more complex behaviours and thus can better fit the data as shown in figure 2.

The increased power of Neural Networks is therefore entirely dependent on the complex relationships within the data. Thus, any claims for improvements in models can only be given on a case by case basis. Traditional scorecards will model data with simple credit risk dependencies just as well as Neural Networks.

The remainder of this paper will detail the three stages envisaged in testing and implementing "New Technology" scorecards.

3   Testing for non-linearity

In the first stage it is necessary to analyse the data to determine whether non-linear modelling techniques (such as Neural Networks) can provide more powerful models than linear techniques (such as Scorecards). This task is relatively trivial to perform; one simply develops a scorecard and Neural Net model (Multi-Layer Perceptron Networks are perhaps the easiest kind of Neural Net to use for this task). If the Neural Net model significantly outperforms the scorecard then one may conclude that there is power to be gained by considering a broader range of models. When building predictive models (including neural networks) several key steps should be followed. These include:

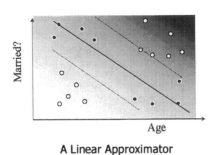

A Linear Approximator

Figure 1: A 2-D data space with a linear approximator.

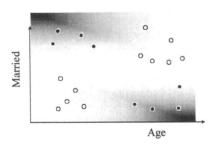

Neural Net model

Figure 2: Same data space with non-linear model illustrated

Identifying suitable development samples: The performance of predictive models depends crucially on the suitability of the development sample. Ideally this sample should be recent, so that the behaviours exhibited are still current, unbiased relative to the current population, and retrospective (i.e. the data that is being used to develop the model is the same as that available at the time the original decisions was made).

Data audit: Before attempting to model a data set simple frequency and distribution statistics should be calculated to ensure that there are no data capture or storage problems.

Characteristic Selection: This problem will be dealt with in more detail in the following section with regard to detailed neural network modelling. For this initial rough test of the non-linearity present within the data a simple technique will suffice. Options include selecting variables that are highly correlated with the good/bad indicator or using stepwise regression techniques.

Avoiding over-fitting: To make valid statistical predictions from any modelling process there must be sufficient data available to make accurate estimates of the parameters in the model. This is a particular problem for neural network architectures due to the relatively large number of free parameters that need to be determined compared to a regression model of the same data set. In order to assess the level of over-fitting, one technique that is commonly employed is to assess the neural networks performance on an independent validation data set. Good performance on the development sample but poor performance on the validation data indicates over-fitting. To avoid developing over-fitted models an extension of this technique is employed where the error on the validation data is continuously monitored during training. Once the error on the validation error starts to rise training is terminated ensuring that the model developed has good generalisation properties.

The graph in figure 3 shows the results of modelling an artificial non-linear data set with scorecards and two different types of Neural Networks. The Neural Networks significantly outperform the scorecards for this (hold-out) data.

Experience on a range of scorecard developments suggest the following rules of thumb apply in real credit risk data:

* Non-linearities are mainly found in data sets that contain behavioural information (i.e. including details of payment histories, balances etc.)
* Modelling non-linearities effectively typically improves the Gini coefficient (a measure of scorecard performance) by around 1-5%. Although small this has a significant impact when aggregated over a large loan portfolio.

Average to large development data sets (7000 records +) with an appreciable proportion of *bads* (at least 5%) are required to detect significant interaction terms. In smaller data sets the interactions cannot be detected against the inherent background noise.

Results from Tests on Non-Linear Data

- **Neural Nets do better than regression**
- **MLPs and RPNs perform similarly**

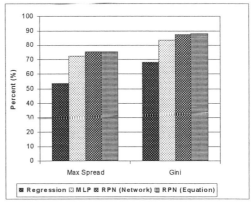

* Both Max Spread and Gini coefficient measure the power of a scoring instrument. See Michie et *al.*(1994) for definitions. The different models are compared in terms of the percentage of correctly classified samples. RPN stands for *Ridge Polynomial Network* (see section 5)

Figure 3: Comparison of performance of different models.

4 Variable selection

In the previous section we examined methods for assessing whether neural network models offer any additional power over scorecard models. Even when the tests have been performed and we have determined that the data at hand does require a full non-linear model, there remain major obstacles to implementing an optimal solution. Perhaps the most immediate problem is to identify which characteristics from the many on offer can be used effectively to predict risk. In traditional linear techniques this question is solved by use of a stepwise regression procedure. This section attempts to identify a suitable analogue to this process for non-linear models.

Selecting an optimal set of variables is a major challenge when modelling consumer behaviour. Its importance arises when trying to avoid two distinct problems:

- Large processing costs
- Over-fitting in the model

In credit and marketing models, the problem is particularly serious because of the large number of variables typically available. The task of a variable selection algorithm is to take a subset of the full set of variables while maintaining all the potential predictiveness of the data. This section will examine the problem of characteristic selection, outlining why traditional algorithms cannot be applied when modelling non-linear data and suggesting how a genetic algorithm can be applied to this problem.

4.1   Breakdown of the problem

In order to understand the variable selection problem, we break it down to examine the broad structure of the task. This will allow us to better compare different methods.

The problem space

The problem space with only four variables
(light = use the variable, dark= don't use it)

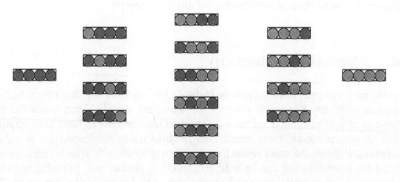

Figure 4: An illustration of the complete search space for a simple four-attribute selection example.

As with many problems, variable selection reduces to a search problem. In other words, we can imagine the search for a solution as an exploration of a problem space. Figure 4 depicts the space of a simple problem with only four variables. Any real variable selection problem is likely to have many more variables and hence a much bigger space. In fact, a problem with n different variables has 2^n possible solutions.

The space illustrated in figure 4 contains one node for every possible subset of the variables. In the illustration, if the ith circle is dark, then the ith variable is present in the subset. Similarly, a light coloured circle indicates that a variable is not present. Thus the picture sets up the space with small subsets on the left and large subsets on the right.

With the space envisaged in this way, we can now consider an algorithm by examining the way in which it searches this space. In what follows there will be four key questions to confront:

- Where do you start the search?
- How do you travel in this space?
- How do you measure a subset's quality?
- When do you stop?

4.2 Traditional selection methods

Exhaustive search

An exhaustive search aims to explore the problem space by examining every possible subset. The obvious flaw in this method is that any genuine variable selection problem will be far too big for the method to be feasible. As an example, consider a typical data set that may have 30 characteristics, it will typically take around 1 minute (being somewhat optimistic) to evaluate a neural network model given an input set of variables. On these rough estimates it would take around 2000 years to evaluate the entire search space!

Stepwise Selection

In this simple algorithm a best guess starting point is chosen for the selected variables. Then each of the unselected variables is added to the model one at a time. The variable that makes the most significant improvement (above some threshold) is selected to enter the subset. Next, each variable in the model is dropped in turn, the one which contributes least to the power of the model is dropped. Repeated cycles of these steps should lead to an improved set of selected variables. The algorithm may settle down to a constant solution or it may cycle around a set of similar quality good solutions.

The advantage of the stepwise technique is that it will converge relatively quickly. It is generally used in combination with a linear model. The linear model is used to develop candidate solutions and thereby evaluate the power of particular variable subsets. This technique should yield near optimal solutions for linear data sets.

By extension, once we try to model non-linear data we clearly want a non-linear model within the stepwise variable selection technique. This on its own however, does not guarantee that an optimal subset of variables is selected. To see this consider a pair of variables A and B, which individually add no power to the model, but contribute significantly in combination. The problem with a stepwise technique is that by adding or removing one variable at a time we will never see any improvement, thus there is no chance of discovering the benefit obtained when both variables are included together. This is an extreme example, however it is representative of the kind of behaviour we are expecting from interacting pairs of variables seen earlier. Because of this problem no stepwise procedure can hope to catch all pair-wise or higher order interactions. To circumvent this problem a development of the Genetic Algorithm called Population Based Incremental Learning (PBIL) is used to find the best subset of variables to enter a model[1]. This is described briefly in the next section.

4.3   Genetic Algorithms & PBIL

Genetic algorithms mimic the process of Darwinian evolution. They generate an increasingly 'good' population of solutions by subjecting these solutions to a process of survival of the fittest. In the context of a particular problem, a GA will produce a population of solutions such that the members of successive generations approach the optimal solution. This is achieved by repeatedly combining high quality individuals to produce "children" while discarding low quality individuals from the population.

Before a GA can be used to solve a problem, the problem must be coded into a suitable form. A solution must be represented as a string of fixed length. Furthermore, we need a measure of "fitness", i.e. a function that measures the quality of each solution.

Once the problem is suitably coded, there are three stages in the GA.

Generate an initial population of solutions. This might be done randomly, or it could build on a priori knowledge of the solution space. Each solution in the population must be assigned a fitness value.

Repeatedly update the population by combining existing members to produce new strings and adding the resulting new strings to the population. At the same time, remove the worst two population members (i.e. those with the lowest fitness).

Once some stopping criterion is met, *stop evolving the population.* This process is illustrated by the flowchart in figure 5.

In the PBIL algorithm much the same considerations are pertinent however in this case instead of maintaining an actual population of candidate solutions we simply store and update the distribution of such a population. By doing this we can save considerable memory and processing requirements over the traditional Genetic Algorithm.

Genetic Algorithms for variable selection

A genetic algorithm operates by manipulating a population of solutions. To do this it requires that solutions be coded as strings that can be "bred" in the manner described.

The variable selection problem is particularly amenable to the coding needed by genetic algorithms. Given a set of n variables, each genetic string has n cells, or "genes". Each gene contains a binary value, 0 or 1. A subset is coded simply by including the ith variable if and only if the ith gene has the value "1". Thus, if we have six variables, the string "000001" describes the variable subset containing only the last variable. Similarly the string "111000" describes the subset containing the first three variables.

How Genetic Algorithms work

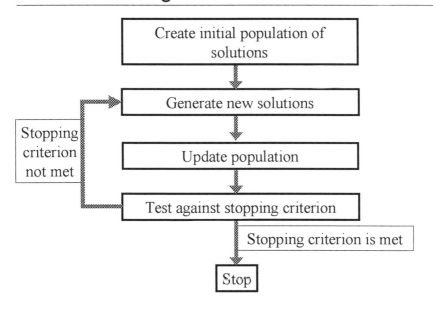

Figure 5: Flowchart of GA optimisation process

4.4   The fitness function

The Radial Basis Function (RBF) neural network will prove useful in the variable selection GA because of its ability to rapidly model non-linear functions. We now look very briefly at the structure of an RBF network. For a more detailed explanation see Bishop[2].

Like most neural networks, the RBF is composed of several layers of nodes. There are three layers: the input layer, hidden layer and output layer. Each of these has a distinct purpose.

The input layer: one node for each variable, used to feed in records.

The hidden layer: in each node, a Gaussian (bell-shaped) function is used to describe a cluster. A record passed from the input layer triggers an activation function if the record is sufficiently similar to the cluster coded by the node.

The output layer: each output node receives input from each node in the hidden layer. The output layer produces a linear combination of the hidden node outputs. These are stored as weights between nodes. The RBF uses these to predict the value of the indicator variable.

Training takes place in two stages. The first stage requires the RBF network to detect clusters in the input data. The second stage occurs once the clusters are identified – at this point, the hidden layer is fixed. The RBF network uses linear algebra to obtain the optimal weights for the output layer. Due to the linear processes in the link between the second and third layers training is very rapid, typically around 10 times quicker than MLP training (in an MLP both output and hidden layer weights must be trained simultaneously).

At this point we have examined how to code variable subsets in an appropriate form, how to breed members of the population together and identified the RBF as an algorithm to evaluate candidate solutions. The final piece is to identify what fitness measure will be used within the GA to rank the quality of the various population members. One of the simplest fitness functions available is to use the error rate of the fully trained RBF network on the validation data set. More sophisticated alternatives are also possible whereby the error rate is balanced against the number of variables so that small models are favoured over large where this does not lead to too great a deterioration in performance. Akaike's Information Criterion (AIC) is one example of such a measure.

4.5　Using variable selection in practice

This section examines the performance of the variable selection GA on credit risk data. The real data was composed of 152 variables together with one indicator. The indicator was a good/bad flag. Some records had values between 0 and 1 indicating an inferred score rather than a known outcome. The training dataset contained 6500 records while the validation dataset contained 3000 records.

As expected, as the GA is allowed to evolve the fitness of the best member of the population begins to improve. In agreement with this observation we can also see in figure 6, that the solutions in the final population have fitness values tightly packed around −1360 while the initial population ranges widely, mostly over lower values.

Of course, it is not clear whether the improvements observed in figure 6 actually justify the processing costs. To examine this further we will build models on the resulting data subset and compare with a model built on the full dataset.

Does the GA population improve?

* Initial and final population

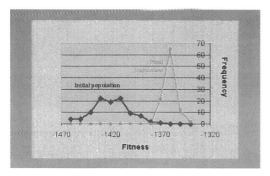

Figure 6: Illustration of GA optimisation in practice.

The results of the variable selection were tested by building a model on a variety of datasets:

* The dataset stripped of a random set of variables
* The dataset stripped of variables not included in the GA solution
* The dataset stripped of variables not included in the stepwise equation
* The full dataset.

A fresh validation sample has been taken in order to ensure a fair comparison. The models were built using a Ridge Polynomial Network (For a description of the RPN model, see next section).

Test using the RPN module   **EQUIFAX**

• **Slightly better than stepwise and full**

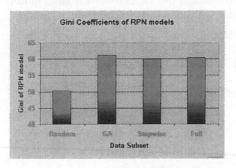

Figure 7: Comparison of different attribute selection methods for use with a neural network model.

The Gini coefficients are plotted in figure 7 for models built on each of four subsets. As expected, a random subset lost much of the power of the data. The stepwise subset produced a model of the same quality as the full dataset. The subset produced by the GA was superior to all of these models. This is likely to be because the GA solution was able to include more variables than the stepwise solution without introducing excessive amounts of noise. This result corroborates the evidence gathered from earlier tests on artificial data. The result here is particularly encouraging since the data had only weak non-linearity.

5   Identifying interaction variables

In the previous section we examined a method for isolating a near optimal selection of variables from which to predict an applicant's credit risk in a non-linear domain. This section identifies a method of isolating exactly which characteristics are interacting. This then allows interaction terms to be entered explicitly into a scorecard model.

One technique that is widely used to allow scorecards to model non-linear data is the use of interaction variables. These provide a mapping of the problem from a space where the goods/bads are not linearly separable to a new space where one hopes they are. In principle, given sufficient interaction terms, any non-linear problem may be mapped to a linear problem, which is then amenable to scorecard modelling. The key issue now is to find an effective method for determining the most efficient interaction variables to use.

The Ridge Polynomial Network (RPN) is a novel neural network architecture developed at the University of Texas by Shin & Ghosh[3]. It has been shown to possess similar modelling properties to the more familiar MLP neural network architecture, in particular it is a "universal approximator". The chief advantage of RPNs over other Neural Network techniques is the ability to extract a polynomial equation from the trained network that can (to an arbitrary level of accuracy) reproduce the neural network model. The first order terms of this polynomial simply reflect the model that would be fitted from a normal logistic regression model. It is the second and higher order terms that are of particular interest since these can be directly interpreted as the necessary interaction terms for a logistic regression solution. Figure 8 illustrates the power of this method on a non-linear problem.

Extracting interaction variables

- Extract polynomial equation
- Automatically build interaction variables
- Construct new regression solution.

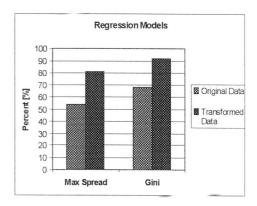

Figure 8: An example of the power of extracted interaction variables.

Much of the original power of the neural net can be recovered with the use of a few dozen interaction terms. This methodology provides a very powerful way of utilising the power of Neural Network techniques while maintaining all the benefits of a standard scorecard approach. The final scorecard model can be built in the normal way allowing the interaction variables detected to step into the models where they meet the relevant significance criteria. The authors have conducted several pilot studies in which the resulting interaction terms have added extra power to the decision making process. Further work is required to determine if there are any common interactions between variables that occur regularly across the majority of products and portfolios when predicting consumer risk.

6   Summary

In this study we have reviewed why neural networks can provide more powerful models than standard scorecards if the underlying data contain non-linearities (or "reversals"). We have then gone on to consider ways of testing data for non-linearities. If non-linearities are detected in a data set we need to find a way of modelling them successfully. The next section therefore identified a scheme for selecting variables for use with neural network models. This method leads to marked performance enhancements over neural net models built with variables selected by stepwise regression techniques. Finally, the role of Ridge Polynomial Networks in detecting interaction terms has been explained. These interaction terms allow scorecards to explicitly model the data sets' non-linearities and thereby allow the final neural net optimised scorecard to roughly equal the power of the best neural network.

Use of these kinds of technique should enable the development of more powerful scorecard risk assessment models in the future. Where previously researchers have assumed that the choice was between the competing methodologies of scorecards or neural networks, here we have attempted to show how these modelling methods may be unified to produce a solution with benefits from both.

Acknowledgements

The authors would like to acknowledge the significant technical contributions of the following individuals in the development of the techniques described herein: Eric Feuilleaubois, Irene White, John Gooday and Valentine Fontama.

References

1. Baluja. 1994. Population Based Incremental Learning. Carnegie Mellon University, Technical Report CMU-CS-94-163.

2. C.M. Bishop. 1995. *Neural Networks for Pattern Recognition*. (Oxford University Press).

3. Y. Shin and J. Ghosh. 1995. Ridge Polynomial Networks. *IEEE Trans. Neural Networks*, **6**(2), 610-622.

Chapter 7

Strategies for Exploiting Neural Networks in Retail Finance

Inderjit Sandhu
Barclays Bank Plc.
E-mail: Inderjit.Sandhu@barclays.co.uk

1   Introduction

" Like a thousand insect-eyes glimmering in shadow, they are watching you. Not Big Brother, quite. Rather, hordes of little brothers gathering scraps of data - each of these, in itself, harmless and dull. Note that bar-code on our front cover, which, combined with a credit-card at the newsagent's desk, could reveal when, where and by whom this newspaper was bought. Need a list of single male camping enthusiasts who live in high income areas and read poetry? It can be had for the asking. ...those glimmering eyes can also be prying, even sinister. "

> *The Economist, 10 February 1996*

Each and every business wants to:

- Contact the customer at the right time with the right product or service at the right price.
- Ensure that customer is always satisfied and never leaves them.
- Manage its cost base and pricing strategy so that customers and products are profitable.

Most organisations hold large quantities of data on their products, and buying behaviours of their customers. The challenge they face is how to turn this data into useful information. The reality is that most organisations are better at collecting data then they are at using it in a sensible way. The amount of data that they collect outstrips their ability to exploit it with their existing methods and processses[1].

The decision-makers want the mountains of data that is held on the databases transformed into information that will help them understand the underlying trends and issues. They want to be able to probe in and look for the underlying relationships and simulate different business scenarios.

Currently in most organisations, most if not all the effort goes into extracting the data from operational databases which is then placed into some kind of a data warehouse. Canned database queries are run for producing regular reports. Primitive tools with limited analysis capability are provided for ad-hoc analysis by the business users. This is not what is needed. Far too much time is spent in organisations producing colourful diagrams on glossy paper which contain very little of what can be described as true information, i.e. information that can be turned quickly into competitive advantage.

The emphasis should be on discovering patterns - ideally 90% of the effort should be on discovering relationships in data and only 10% on data maintenance. Effective use of technology and business processes should go a long way in achieving this target.

2   Some business questions to consider before thinking about technology

It is very tempting to start considering a technology, almost always one that has not been used before by an organisation without paying adequate attention to some fundamental business questions.

The customer now belongs to the enterprise. The customer's needs are being met via multiple channels and with multiple products. Customers move dynamically in and out of target groups for each product.

If we accept that the customer belongs to the enterprise then it implies that the business has to have an efficient way of capturing, storing and distributing sales and service information. The enterprise has to ensure that all salespeople (field force, service centres etc.) know all about the customer. Team selling and service becomes the critical success factor for the enterprise.

In our view, the analysis should always start by understanding:

- How is customer profitability defined?
- How do we acquire new customers cost effectively?
- How can we increase the profitability of existing customers - both in terms of revenue and reduction in cost?
- How do we ensure that the customer remains with us?
- How does pricing, promotion, channel and product drive customer behaviour?
- Is it possible to attribute and measure customer behaviour to an initiative? This needs to be more than the traditional market share, sales volumes etc. Focus should be on profitability, cross selling, customer value etc.
- What do we wish to know about our customers, products and delivery channels? Why?
- How do we plan to exploit this information? It is worthwhile running through scenarios on how the information will be exploited, as it tends to highlight new opportunities and problems early.
- What are the potential problems?
- What data do we have and how can this be supplemented? Where is the data stored and who owns it? What is the format of data - not by field but its nature. As an example, in a service centre a lot of useful information may be held in contact history files which are written in free text. Perhaps, the first clues of a dissatisfied customer may be in these files.

Thus the focus should be on people, technology and business processes and how they will enable a business solution - not the "wiz-bang" of any particular technology. This is difficult since users, first hear of a technology from vendors who naturally want to emphasis their product and its feature. Business users are far too often reactive and very rarely proactive. A well managed, proactive approach saves time and reduces costs. To be effective it needs senior executive support.

3 Data

The issues relating to data can be categorised into:

- Quality
- Representation
- Legal requirements

Quality and representation
The foremost question is the quality of data. This includes accuracy and completeness. Quantity should not be taken for granted. All modelling techniques need representative samples.

Some of the issues are:

- How easy is it to extract it? Can the process be automated?
- Is the data at the transaction level or has it been summarised?
- If the data set contains a mixture of numeric - continuous and discrete and non-numeric then is there any significance in this representation? How will this be represented in the model? Tools exist to ease experimentation.
- How complete / sparse is the data set? This should not be based on a simple analysis but a careful study of the data set. As an example, is there a combination of attributes for which data is very sparse?
- What are the known dynamics in the business environment? How are they likely to be exhibited in the data set? What potential relationships may exist?
- What is the complexity of the information that this data may hold?

As an example, suppose it is necessary to build an application to detect credit card fraud. There are large volumes of data (millions of transactions each day), but only a small fraction are potential fraud cases. Thus the data is highly skewed. The length of the transactional history for each cardholder will be of variable length. The loss from each fraud will vary. How should this modelled? Is there sufficient data to build, validate and test the model?

Legal requirements
There are legal requirements on data protection that must be met. As an example, the OCED guidelines[2] are:

- Collection limitation - data needs to be collected lawfully, where possible with the consent of the subject.
- Data quality - must be complete, accurate and up to date.
- Purpose of the data usage -must be specified prior to collection.
- Disclosure - the data should not be disclosed without legal cause or consent.
- Security - Data should be protected.
- Openness - on what data is stored and the subject should be able to correct any inaccuracies.

One of the big differences is that in Europe, certain classes of data are seen as inherently private, whilst in US, privacy is defined by the context in which data is used. These are difficult and sensitive issues as increasingly more information is shared within an organisation and the volume of transactions across legal borders is increasing rapidly. E-commerce is posing a number of challenges on how to protect confidentiality of private information.

4 Matching problems and technology

4.1 Technology selection

Before any technology is selected, a matrix of the type shown in table 1 should be completed and maintained. Matching business problem to technology is an iterative process and should be pro-actively managed. Otherwise it becomes very much a "knee-jerk" reactive type of analysis and the resulting decisions are always sub-optimal.

The purpose of this is to create a framework for decision making. The various factors need to carefully considered and a "balanced judgement call needs to be made" on which technologies should be explored further.

The important point here is that there is no single globally optimal solution that is obvious for any given problem. It is important to think laterally but this needs to be done in the context of the environment.

Potential technologies that could be used	
In-house understanding of technology	
Availability and maturity of tools	
Skills and experience	
Case studies of using technology	
Case studies of using technology to solve similar problems	
Probability of success	
Likely costs and time scales	
Risks	
Unknowns at this stage	

Table 1: Matrix including the nature of the business problem: This needs to be described in generic terms and then specifics.

A simple example: Credit card fraud detection
The business problem is to reduce credit card fraud. As an over simplification, data is available on the personal details of the cardholder, payment history, history of transactions, etc.

A potential range of technologies include:

1. Neural Networks[3,4,5]
2. Knowledge Based Systems
3. Rule Induction
4. Data Mining[6]
5. Knowledge Discovery
6. Chi-square Automatic Interaction Detection (CHAID)
7. Data Visualisation[7,8,9]
8. Cased Based Reasoning
9. Genetic Algorithms[10]
10. Fuzzy Logic[20]
11. Clustering techniques
12. "Classical" Statistical techniques

Even if the analysts know nothing about Neural Networks, the fact that a product exists[3,4] for the vertical market means that this technology should be explored further. Another important point is that there is a range of technologies, each with its strengths and weaknesses. Any decision has got to take into account an organisation underlying skills and how effective they currently are at tackling the problem. This is not a limiting factor, but it helps in determining the way forward.

Thus using the above technologies as a starting point, completing the matrix in table 1 will raise a number of questions and issues. These need to be explored in an iterative fashion and the range of options will narrow. Ideally, it would be worthwhile to try out at least two approaches so that it is possible to compare and contrast. This is not as expensive as it sounds. The main limitations in being able to explore a range of options are the technical skills of the analysis team and whether they operate on re-active or pro-active basis.

4.2 Tools selection

All the common criteria such as local support, availability of training etc apply. The other factors that need to be considered for tool selection are:

- Data Access: How easy is it to access the various databases that are in use? Does the tool access the database or is it necessary first to extract the data into some sort of intermediary database.
- Pre-processing: It is always necessary to carry out pre-processing and, depending on the technology, this can take more than a third of the total effort. What pre-processing aids are provided? In building a Neural Network model, the choice of pre-processing will be one of the most significant factors in determining the final performance of the model. At it's simplest, it may just be a transformation of input data, or it may be used to reduce the dimensionality of the input data.
- Range of Techniques Supported: Clearly an assessment of this depends on the cost of the tools. One of the important factors here is the extent that the tools allow the user to adopt the model. What data visualisation tools are supplied?
- Testing Aid: It will be necessary to assess a model performance on a validation data set. What aids are provided by the tool to compare different models? How easy is to understand and validate the model?
- Implementation and Scale-up: How easy will it be the implementation of the solution in a production environment? Will the solution scale up? Will the tool scale up to larger volumes of data?

4.3 Skills

Apart from the basic technical skills, the team needs to have skills in:

- A deep understanding of the domain.
- Desire to continuously learn.
- Structure experimentation.

4.4 Factors that impact technology adoption

Some of the main factors that act as a drag on adoption of Neural Networks and other pattern recognition technologies are:

- *Quality of data*: There is simply no substitute for quality.
- *Skills*: The analysis team needs to have a deep understanding of the domain, statistical and computing skills.
- *Senior Management Support*: The team needs to have active management support. This function needs to be pro-active. A small, well managed team can achieve a great deal - though clearly the size of the team depends on a number of organisational factors.
- *Cost of Experimentation*: The cost of tools for experimentation can be relatively modest. One of the largest factors on cost and time is the existing skills base.

- *Measurement of Success:* A degree of experimentation is necessary. By the sheer nature of experimentation, success cannot be guaranteed first time and every time. In some domains, it can be difficult to measure precisely the contribution of the various factors that lead to business success.
- *Terminology:* The use of "different words" to describe similar concepts may be great for drawing attention to a technology but in general tends to inhibit technology adoption over a longer period. Metaphors are a powerful tool for getting ideas across – however, if not used carefully, they can mislead and almost act as barriers for technology adoption.

R.G.Fichman & F. Kemere[11] have defined several factors, represented in figure 1, that impact any new technology adoption.

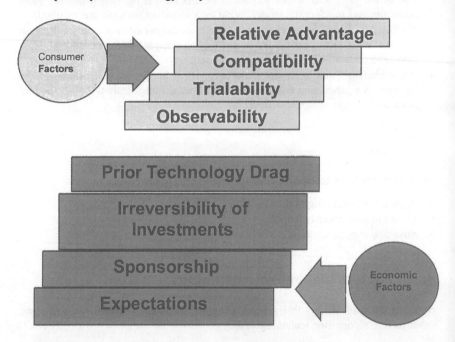

Figure 1: Factors that impact the adoption of new technologies

5   A short case study: credit risk assessment

The purpose of this case study is to illustrate the points made in this paper. The case study has been deliberately simplified - as an example, details of pre-processing have been omitted. Various pre-processing and cost functions are covered in all good books on Neural Networks[5] and Machine Learning.

The business challenge is correct classification of individuals for credit risk assessment. The current approach is based on "standard statistical techniques".

For each customer, data is available on:

- Personal details
- Financial information
- Credit history

A large data set is available for building, validating and testing the models. Testing should not be taken lightly. After all the goal of the model is not to memorise the training set but to be able to predict when a new data set is presented. A range of approaches for testing models is described in the literature.
The first set of questions that needs to be considered is:

- What is the potential range of technologies?
- Which technology should be trailed?
- Will it be possible to implement in a high volume, fast though put environment?

Analysis of the technical literature result in the following candidate technologies:
- Neural Networks[3,4,5,14]
- Rule Induction[12]
- Genetic Algorithms
- K-Nearest Neighbour (K-NN)
- Data Visualisation
- Knowledge Based Systems

It is decided not to pursue with:

- Knowledge Based Systems. The team has extensive experience and knowledge of Statistics and feels that building a knowledge-based system would be time consuming and risky. Their assessment is that they would need to represent uncertainty in their KBS and it is not obvious to them how this can be done quickly.
- Data Visualisation[7,8,9]. This could provide them with a better insight into their data. At present the team feels far more comfortable at analysis data in tabular form rather than data presented visually. Data visualisation is skill that they currently lack and they decided to develop this outside this exercise.

Rule Induction

It is claimed by Gantiv *et al.*[13] that decision trees are attractive in data-mining environments for several reasons:

- Their intuitive representation makes the resulting classification model easy to understand.
- Constructing decision trees does not require any input parameters from the analysts.
- The predictive accuracy of decision trees is equal to or higher than other classification models.

The performance of rule induction on the test set was poor. Only 60% of the outputs were correctly classified. The major weakness was that the algorithms do not permit guidance from the domain expert during the search process.

In addition, risk assessment teams demand statistical rigor and confidence bounds which the standard rule-induction techniques can not provide.

Genetic Algorithm
The results from the Genetic Algorithm were only marginally better than rule induction. It was difficult for the domain expert to interpret a number of the rules that the system generated.

Neural Networks
Neural networks are inherently suitable for modelling non-linear relationships in data. A "relatively standard" approach for the pre-processing and the topology of the back propagation algorithm yielded 68% accuracy. Refinements to the pre-processing and the topology improved the performance to 73%.

It was decided to experiment with the *mixture of experts* model[15]. The underlying philosophy of the model is that, if the tasks can be decomposed into subtasks, it is sensible for the learner to have a modular structure in which each module is a local expert that learns to perform one or more of the subtasks. The identification of subtasks and the assignment of experts to subtasks are part of the learning problem.

This model performed the best on the test data - yielding 79% of accuracy. There was noise in the data and no model was expected to do better than about 85%.

Having concluded that Neural Networks are better at this problem for this type of data, the next stage is to:

- Select the most suitable Neural Network model - as stated earlier, the goal is not to see which model learns the data best but which model gives the best generalisation and adopts quickly to changes in the environment[16,19]
- For risk assessment, and this is not the case for marketing, there is a need to understand the reasons for a decision. It is possible to obtain a "limited reasoning" by keeping the model simple and carrying out sensitivity analysis[17,18].

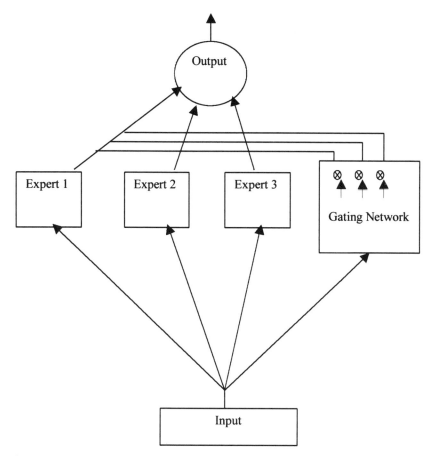

Figure 2: Representation of the mixture of experts model. The gating network acts as a switch - it decides which of the expert networks will be used for a given input.

6   Conclusions

The customer now really belongs to the enterprise - served via multiple channels. The customer is touched by a number of functions and they must share information.

A customer model now means integrating marketing databases with information from sales, marketing initiatives, product availability, customer services and accounting information. It is one thing to build a data warehouse but it is a major challenge to develop techniques and strategies to exploit it.

The development of the strategy should begin by examining and understanding the critical factors and how they interact with business problems. A successful technology-enabled strategy hinges on an objective evaluation of critical vendors, architectures, applications and infrastructures as they are applied to the business functions.

Architecture for analytical analysis needs to be developed. Neural Networks are a key technology in this architecture. To fully exploit it, the team needs to be pro-active and have good technical and domain skills. It needs to be part of the tool kit.

Neural Networks are not and can not be a panacea. They are very effective at modelling complex patterns but their effectiveness depends on the quality of data and technical skills of the analysts.

References

1. D. Waltz and S.J. Hong. 1999. Data mining: a long term dream. *IEEE Intelligent Systems*, 4(6), 30-31.

2. http:/www.oecd.org/dsti/iccp/lgal/priv-en.html

3. PRISM family of Products Nestor Inc. (http:/www.nestor.com)

4. Falcon and Eagle products from HNC

(http:// www.hncfs.com/products/riskmanage.htm)

5. C.M.Bishop. 1995. *Neural Networks for Pattern Recognition*. (Oxford University Press)

Data Mining in *IEEE Computer*, August 1999, 34-75.

6. E.R.Tufte. 1983. *The Visual Display of Quantitative Information*. (Graphics Press)

7. P.R. Keller and M.M.Keller. 1993. *Visual Cues - Practical Data Visualisation*. (IEEE Computer Society Press)

8. D.W. Scott. 1992. *Multivariate Density Estimation: Theory, Practice and Visualisation*. (John Wiley)

9. D.E. Goldberg. 1989. *Genetic Algorithms in Search, Optimisation and Machine Learning*. (Addison-Wesley)

10. R.G. Fichman and C.F. Kemerer. 1993. Solan Management Review

11. J. Quinlan J. 1993. *C 4.5 Program for Machine Learning*. (Morgan Kanfuman)

12. V. Ganti, J. Gehrke and R. Ramakrishnan 1999. Mining very large databases. *IEEE Computer*, 32(8), 38-45.

13. T. Kohonen. 1989. *Self-Organisation and Associative Memory* (3rd Edition, Springer-Verlag)

14. R. Jacobs, M.I. Jordon, S.J. Nowlan and G.E. Hinton. 1991. Adaptive mixtures of local experts. *Neural Computation*, 3(1), 79-87.

15. J.M. Twomey and A.E. Smith. 1998. Bias and variance of validation methods for function approximation neural networks under conditions of sparse data. *IEEE transactions on Systems, Man and Cybernetic*, **28**(3), 417-430.

16. T. Corbett-Clark and L. Tarasssenko. 1997. A principled framework and technique for rule extraction from multi-layer perceptrons. In *Proc. 5th IEE Int. Conf. On Artificial Neural Networks*, Cambridge: U.K., 233-238.

17. R. Setiono. 1997. Extracting rules from Neural Networks by pruning and hidden unit splitting. *Neural Computation*, **9**, 205-225.

18. T. Heskes. 1997. Practical confidence and prediction intervals. In *Advances in Neural Information Processing Systems*, **9**, 176-182.

19. J.C. Bezdek and S.K. Pal. (eds.) 1992. Fuzzy Models for Pattern Recognition: Methods That Search for Structures in Data.

Chapter 8

Novel Techniques for Profiling and Fraud Detection in Mobile Telecommunications

John Shawe-Taylor and Keith Howker
Royal Holloway, University of London.
E-mail: john@dcs.rhbnc.ac.uk; jkh@dcs.rhbnc.ac.uk

Phil Gosset, Vodafone Ltd

Mark Hyland, Herman Verrelst and Yves Moreau
Katholieke Universiteit Leuven

Christof Stoermann, Siemens AG

Peter Burge, Logica UK Ltd

1   Introduction

This chapter, some of which has appeared in an earlier article[1], looks at some of the results of a work done in the CEC's *ACTS*[a] programme by the collaborative R&D project *ASPeCT*[b]. The project was set up to look at the problems and solutions for security in third generation mobile telecommunications systems– UMTS[c] – which will follow on from GSM. UMTS offers much greater data rates, and hence the possibility of a wide range of services that will be heavily dependent on comprehensive security facilities. The project consortium consisted of Network Operators (Vodafone, Panafon), equipment suppliers (Siemens ATEA, Siemens AG, Giesecke & Devrient) and academic institutions (Royal Holloway, University of London and Katholieke Universiteit Leuven). While the greater part of the project focussed on protection of the communications between the users and their

---

[a] Advanced Communications, Technologies and Services (DG XIII/B)
[b] Advanced Security for Personal Communications Technologies – completed 31-JAN-1999
[c] Universal Mobile Telecommunications System

service providers, network operators and value-added services – mainly related to cryptographic mechanisms and services – a substantial section addressed the problems of fraud and abuse of the networks, looking at possible tools for detection and management, and also examining the legal implications for the technical approach.

This chapter concerns only the fraud-related work. It examines the viability of the tools that were designed and implemented and gives an overview of some of the legal findings.

It has been estimated that the mobile communication industry is currently losing many millions of Euros per year to fraud and abuse, so prevention and early detection of malicious activity is an important goal. It is clear that the additional security measures taken in GSM and being planned for the future UMTS systems make these networks less vulnerable to fraud than the previous analogue generation. Nevertheless, certain types of commercial fraud will remain difficult to preclude by technical means alone. Some of these types of fraud will be described below. It is probably true that it is impossible to eliminate fraud totally, but the use of advanced fraud management techniques can assist in early detection and classification of incidents, and will also reduce the scope and effectiveness of technical frauds.

The problem is an economic one: the objective is to minimise the cost of protection against abuse plus actual loss due to the abuse. The fraud detection regime has to remain cost effective in a competitive environment where the fraudster will continue to try to devise new means to beat the system.

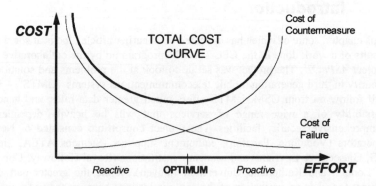

Figure 1: Cost Analysis of anti-Fraud Measures

Figure 1 shows the relationship between the cost of fraud and countermeasures versus the performance of the fraud detection tool. As efforts are increased to counter fraud the cost of the countermeasures becomes increasingly expensive to the point where the cost of the countermeasure could be far greater than the cost of the remaining fraud. The thicker Total Cost Curve shows the two graphs summed to indicate an optimum, most cost-effective level.

The power of Neural Networks (NN) as tools for discrimination, recognition and classification is well known, therefore this seems a natural technique to apply to the problem of detecting and identifying fraudulent activity.

The use of modern AI techniques is not new in fraud detection; substantial AI expertise has been brought to bear in the area of credit card transaction fraud detection. The problem there is in many respects more straightforward than for mobile telecoms. For instance there is only one type of fraud and only one type of transaction, in contrast with the large number of mobile phone fraud scenarios, some of which are outlined below, together with the different types of calls and call information that can be monitored in fraud detection. Hence, a straightforward application of the solution strategy developed for credit card fraud is neither feasible nor would it be effective. The work here concerned the task of studying the problem of fraud detection in mobile telecoms, of identifying the relevant fraud scenarios, determining the resulting fraud indicators and of designing and demonstrating novel techniques that are effective state-of-the-art solutions to the problem

The techniques developed are based on the fact that attempts at fraud or other abuse of the network's services by a user are always going to display some significant behaviour characteristics that differ from previous patterns of legitimate activity. The recognition, and possibly classification, of such differences or changes is the challenge that the project set itself.

2 Fraud scenarios

Many new frauds have appeared since the project was started in late 1995. Much of this has been due to the introduction of pre-payment schemes (which were introduced not least to limit opportunity for fraud). We outline some of the more important scenarios below, and identify others. Non pre-payment fraud includes the following:

Subscription fraud
This is by far the most common fraud encountered on the GSM network. A person uses false identification to obtain a service with no intention of paying the bill. The dedicated fraudster will attempt to maximise the potential revenue to be made by obtaining as much service as possible, e.g. by claiming to be a small business requiring multiple subsidised handsets. Subscription fraud is a fraud in its own right but is also a means to committing further frauds such as running a call sell operation, premium rate frauds (see below) or just providing another link in a complex chain of call redirection, to hide oneself, as part of a call sell operation.

PBX fraud

Many companies provide a dial-through service via their PBX system so that authorised employees can use it for business purposes such as making international calls from wherever they may be located. This service is open to abuse if a fraudster obtains the password for such a system. The key problem with PBX frauds is the security weaknesses introduced into the system by the inexperienced or careless administrator. Passwords for PBX systems are often left as the default. Once the fraudster has established the PBX equipment type, he tries the default password. Sometimes a fraudster has 'shoulder surfed' in order to see an employee keying in the password. If all else fails, the fraudster will try a simple war dialling approach of making many short duration back-to-back calls, systematically trying to guess the password. These calls tend to occur out of office hours and are to fixed landline numbers. Note that this technique can be automated using simple dial-out software.

Freephone fraud and call-back fraud

Freephone fraud and call-back fraud are special cases and could also be considered as a provision for fair competition in a deregulated market place, however in some countries it is illegal. With both, an operator's network resources are being used with the operator gaining little or no revenue for the call.

If free calls can be made to freephone call resellers access points, calls can be made at lower rates that are normally associated with wireline calls. The call reseller does not have to be concerned about the mobile element of the call. With call-back fraud, an access number is dialled, the call dropped and a subsequent call back received presenting to the caller a dial tone, from where the caller can dial on. The operator only receives the cost of the inbound call, whilst the call reseller picks up the profit on the international leg (say).

Premium rate service (PRS) fraud

Premium rate services can be abused in various ways. For example a person could set up a premium rate line with a national operator. The operator is obliged to pay the owner of the line a proportion of the revenue generated. The fraudster then uses a fraudulent mobile to dial this number for long periods. He would also attempt to get other people to do the same. The fraudster then pockets the revenue without paying for the calls. Premium rate services can be abused is by setting up a fraudulent mobile to divert calls to a popular premium rate line. The caller then only pays normal rates whilst the fraudulent mobile picks up the tab at the premium rate. Characteristics are long back-to-back calls.

Handset theft

The theft of an intermittently used phone can result in significant revenue loss before the phone is registered as being stolen. More frequently now, especially with pre-pay, distribution depots are being hit in ram raids by organised gangs. The handsets can then be unlocked and exported.

Roaming fraud

This is when a fraudster makes use of the delays in the transfer of Toll Tickets through roaming on a foreign network or through using a foreign SIM on a UK network, say. (Technically the latter should be called 'visitor fraud'.) Weekend usage presented a very reliable delay in the past. Such delays are fortunately being reduced by modern billing systems.

Other scenarios include *Fax-back and malicious call-back fraud, Technical internal fraud, Mobile to mobile fraud, Tumbling fraud and Hijacking.* More information on these and other aspects of this note may be found on the project's web-site[2].

In addition a new family of scenarios has grown around *pre-payment* – itself meant as a counter to some of the above. Due to the infancy of this technology there are a number of obvious and not so obvious loopholes that enable fraudsters to make money. This mainly revolves around the voucher scheme whereby a person walks into a shop and purchases air-time via a physical voucher. The voucher contains a code number that when entered into the phone enables calls to be made; our fraudster is in business again. Identified instances include *Cheque fraud, Credit card fraud, Voucher theft, Voucher ID duplication, Faulty vouchers, Network access fraud, Network attack, Long duration calls, Handset theft, and Roaming fraud.*

Future frauds

Recently a rather grey fraud has started to appear. Multiple heavily discounted pre-pay handsets are being purchased in the UK at supermarkets and other outlets, quite legitimately. These handsets are never registered on the UK network and are exported to countries where no handset subsidy exists. Once the phones have been 'hacked' to unlock them, they are a valuable commodity. Essentially, no fraud has been committed?

With the dawn of mobile commerce, more and more companies will offer this means of doing business. Operators are going to witness very rapid growth in the use of their SMS service. It is essential that operators start to profile their customer's use of this service in a similar manner to the voice service. Banks, for example, will expect operators to be fully compliant with their security requirements. With mobile commerce, unlike Internet commerce, secure transaction technology through encryption is not yet available.

WAP is becoming the defacto standard now for applications interfacing to mobile technology. Gaining illegitimate access to an operator's WAP server gateway will be highly desirable to the fraudster. These server gateway's and ISP services which operators are being drawn into offering all need to be considered for future fraud detection purposes.

3   The fraud detection environment

There are three main roles that need to be considered in the Fraud Detection Environment. The first is the User, the entity that makes calls on the network. The User has a contractual relationship with the second entity, the Service Provider (SP), who charges the User for the calls that are made. The third entity is the Network Operator (NO) who sells blocks of air-time to the SP for selling on to the User. There is no direct contract between the NO and the User.

The purpose of a fraud detection system, or more specifically the Fraud Detection Tool (FDT) is to detect fraudulent behaviour of Users from their usage data before the cost of such activity becomes too great. To achieve this, it is clear that the tool should be placed where it can receive this usage data as quickly as possible. This means that the FDT should optimally be closely connected to the Network.

Within the Network, there are two possible sources of usage data that can be employed for Fraud Detection. The first source is the Toll Tickets (or Call Detail Records - CDRs), the records of the calls produced for billing purposes, generally constructed immediately the call has finished. The second source is the Signalling Data that is produced in the network.

The advantage of using Signalling Data is that it makes more usage information available. For example, the location of the User at every Location Update would be available, as well as the opportunity to monitor the set-up of a call when it happens, rather than only once the call is finished. However, the disadvantage is the sheer volume of output, one or two orders of magnitude greater than that produced for billing, which would make impossible filtering and processing demands on the monitoring system.

The advantage of using the Toll Tickets (TTs) is that the information that is produced for billing also contains usage behaviour information valuable for Fraud Detection. However, billing data needs to be gathered securely, and not necessarily quickly, so data may be a day old before it is processed. To allow for *hot billing*, where bills can be created very rapidly, and also to minimise this fraud risk window, a mediation device may be included in the network that polls the switches for their TTs on a regular basis. The data thus collected can be considered to be near-real time, as the difference between real time delivery and polled retrieval can be made as small as practicable.

Once the TTs are processed, action needs to be taken in response to any alarms that are raised by the FDT. Such responses could be to question the Users to see if the activity had some benign rationale. However, there is a problem: there is no direct contract between the User and the NO[a], so the alarms will need to be distributed to the relevant SPs, and they will take appropriate action.

---

[a] The organization operating the network is now tending also to have Service Supplier operations

3.1 System requirements

Performance
To minimise fraud losses, it is important that the FDT operate as close to real-time as possible. Using a mediation device to provide such a feed has another consequence, that of smoothing processing requirements. However, the usage of the Network varies throughout the day, and there will be a 'busy hour' in the day which may contains 15% of the day's traffic. The system will need to process tickets at a rate in line with this value.

Customisation
The FDT must be easily tuneable for customisation of fraud detection sensitivity and for alarm filtering.

Scalability and flexibility
The FDT must be scaleable and adaptable in the fast growing mobile network environment. That would mean that any thresholds set during the initialisation period should not reduce because of the network expansion. The FDT must also be flexible towards new and changing fraud methods and characteristics (i.e. behaviour changes) that are expected to manifest themselves in the future.

3.2 ASPeCT choice of technology

The ASPeCT tool did not set out to provide a flexible interface, strong database technologies, user friendliness and case management, which marketable products have, but in the later stages of the project, a number of these issues were tackled. The effort required to bring ASPeCT-based product to market would be small.

There are currently over 30 fraud management products on the marketplace. Few appear to have performed a rigorous examination of the artificial intelligence technologies that could be applied to reducing fraud. ASPeCT carried out a thorough survey of options and possibilities in this area.

From our analysis it was clear that a Rule-Based tool is a vital component of the tool-kit for identifying certain frauds. It is a *white box* approach and hence the management system can be given a reason why the tool has flagged an alarm for a particular user - essential for the legalities of barring the user from the network.

However, a Rule-Based tool on its own is not sufficient to deal with the complexities and intricacies of mobile telecoms fraud. Some form of "fuzzy" soft-computing technique is required to handle scenarios that cannot be precisely specified by rules (a situation that is prevalent in mobile fraud, but perhaps less common in other fraud detection areas, such as credit card). Neural Networks provide just this sort of technology able to deal with novel or abnormal instances or scenarios.

Four discrete FDT components were developed by the project:

- a rule based tool;
- a neural network based tool using supervised learning;
- an unsupervised learning tool utilising neural networks looking at A-number data in the toll tickets;
- an unsupervised learning tool utilising neural networks looking at B-number data in the toll tickets.

The four component tools were integrated into a single system FDT which we called BRUTUS[a]. We also built a graphical user interface illustrated in Figure 2, which displays the monitoring information and alarms, and provides management of the rules and parameters of the system.

3.3   User Profiling

The fraud detection tool uses a completely data-driven approach. All the information gathered by the tool comes only from the individual user-specific toll tickets. A method must be found to profile each user and to extract relevant information from the Toll Ticket to try to detect any fraudulent use. It should be noted that no geographical information was used; this could be used to further strengthen the system at a later stage.

Absolute or differential analysis

Toll Tickets are data records containing details of each mobile phone call attempt that is made. Toll Tickets are transmitted to the network operator by the cells or switches that the mobile phone was communicating with at the time.

In addition to providing necessary billing information, Toll Tickets contain additional information that can be used to identify a fraudster. Existing fraud detection systems tend to interrogate sequences of Toll Tickets comparing a function of the various fields with fixed criteria known as *triggers*. A trigger, if activated, raises an alert status that cumulatively would lead to an investigation by the network operator. Such fixed trigger systems perform what is known as an *absolute* analysis of the Toll Tickets and are proficient at detecting the extremes of fraudulent activity.

Another approach to the problem is to perform a *differential* analysis. Here, behavioural patterns of the mobile phone are monitored by comparing its most recent activities with a history of its usage. Criteria can then be derived to use as triggers that are activated when the usage pattern of a mobile phone changes

---

[a] The original rationale for the BRUTUS acronym has been mislaid, but it seemed a nice name to keep for the GUI guard-dog.

significantly over a short period of time. A change in the behaviour pattern of a mobile phone is a common characteristic in nearly all fraud scenarios excluding those committed on initial subscription where there is no behavioural pattern established.

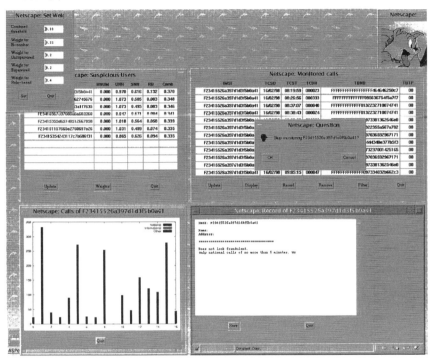

Figure 2: Screenshot of the graphical user interface of the integrated fraud detection system

There are many advantages to performing a differential analysis through profiling the behaviour of a user. Firstly, certain behavioural patterns may be considered anomalous for one type of user, and hence potentially indicative of fraud, but would be considered acceptable for another. With a differential analysis flexible criteria can be developed that detect any change in usage based on a detailed history profile of user behaviour. This takes fraud detection down to the personal level comparing like with like, enabling detection of less obvious frauds that may only be noticed at the personal usage level. An absolute usage system would not detect fraud at this level. In addition, because a typical user is not a fraudster, the majority of criteria that would have triggered an alarm in an absolute usage system will be seen as a large change in behaviour in a differential usage system. In this way a differential analysis can be seen as incorporating the absolute approach.

The differential approach

Most fraud indicators do not become apparent from an individual Toll Ticket. With the possible exception of a velocity trap, confidence can only be gained in detecting a real fraud through investigating a fairly long sequence of Toll Tickets. This is particularly the case when considering more subtle changes in a user's behaviour by performing a differential analysis. All the tools adopt an approach based on analysis of user profiles based on comparison of recent and longer-term behaviour histories derived from the toll ticket data.

A differential usage system requires information concerning the user's history of behaviour plus a more recent sample of the mobile phones activities. An initial approach might be to extract and encode information from Toll Tickets and to store it in record format. This would require two windows or spans over the sequence of transactions for each user. The shorter sequence is called the Current User Profile (CUP) and the longer sequence, the User Profile History (UPH).

Both profiles could be treated and maintained as finite length queues. When a new Toll Ticket arrives for a given user, the oldest entry from the UPH would be discarded and the oldest entry from the CUP would move to the back of the UPH queue. The new record encoded from the incoming Toll Ticket would then join the back of the CUP queue. Clearly it is not optimal to search and retrieve historical information concerning a user's activities prior to each calculation, on receipt of a new Toll Ticket. A more suitable approach is to compute a single cumulative CUP and UPH, for each user, from incoming Toll Tickets that can be stored as individual records, in a database. To maintain the concept of having two different spans over the Toll Tickets without retaining a database record for each Toll Ticket, both profiles need to be decayed before the influence of a new Toll Ticket can be taken into consideration. A profile for each user can then be represented as a probability distribution by normalising the data in the profile. As well as being a very natural approach for the NN components, user profiling helps the rule-based component to overcome its most criticised drawback, the inflexibility of one set of rules applied to all users; user profiles allow a far more flexible, user-specific treatment.

The neural network-based tools use only a differential analysis; the rule based tool also allows absolute analysis against fixed criteria.

3.4   The FDT components

The rule-based tool

The rule-based tool must be initialised with manually set parameters – the *rules*. It can work in two ways: examining the toll ticket data against fixed criteria (absolute mode) and examining them against variations from previous observations (differential mode).

Neural Network based tool using supervised learning

The Supervised learning tool needs to be educated to set up the appropriate configuration of neurons and controlling parameters. Before exposure to the data for investigation, the system is fed a set of training data to initialise the system, and then a set of validation data to confirm the correctness of the set up. The system is now ready to process the operational toll tickets.

Unsupervised learning tool utilising neural networks

An unsupervised Neural Network is used to look at how a user's behaviour changes over time. It needs no prior knowledge of fraud, unlike the previous two tools. There are two Unsupervised Neural Networks used in BRUTUS. An A-Number analysis, which detects changes in the users' behaviour on the phone, and an international B-Number analysis, which looks at specific changes in behaviour of a user making international calls.

Brutus

These four AI tools are integrated together to form the complete ASPeCT Fraud Detection Tool – BRUTUS as in Figure 3. Each tool can detect separately suspicious looking or unusual behaviour and raise an alarm appropriately. A GUI has also been implemented for easy user management. For the prototype system it is run via a web browser. The GUI can keep track of suspicious users and allows the operator to look at a specific user's calls to give the final decision whether they should be subject to further action.

The system operates by cascading the input data stream through the sequence of tools:

- The Unsupervised NN: very good for novelty detection; good negative predictive value, which means that they can eliminate those users very easily for which certainly nothing is untoward; therefore used as a first filter to all incoming calls; a further reason for putting these modules high up in the chain is that their profiling could possibly also be used as input to the Supervised NN. Two unsupervised NNs are deployed:

- B-number analysis: adding information on the destination of international calls will be able to boost the already reported performance of the individual tools; this module comes first because it adds information to the data-stream that could easily be used by all three subsequent tools.

- A-number analysis: carries out the general surveillance of toll tickets for significant fluctuations in user behaviour; as there is no training or rule set up, this tool can also recognise genuinely novel activity possibly characteristic of a new type or variant of attack.

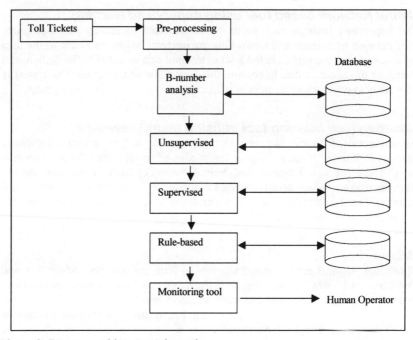

Figure 3: BRUTUS architecture schematic

- The Supervised NN: efficiently pinpoints users whose behaviour is similar to previously observed and recorded fraudulent behaviour; its training routines can be tuned to bias the performance towards a high positive predictive value, i.e. when it puts a fraudulent label on a user, the subsequent modules and/or human operator can be confident that there really is something of concern.
- The Rule Based system: does very well in explaining why alarms have been raised; it could, for example, be extended with extra rules to inspect why previous modules had raised an alarm; in this fashion, new fraud scenarios can possibly be identified; it can also be used to define hyper-rules based on alarms raised by other tools and not only on its own profiling/information.

The outline operation of the integrated tool is shown in figure 4. Outputs are passed via the database and *monitoring evaluation unit* to the monitoring tool which displays its alarms to the human operator.

4   The ASPeCT trial[3]

One of the difficulties of running a convincing user-trial of our prototype system was obtaining sufficient toll ticket data. Great care had to be taken by network operators in *sanitizing* all data passed to us in order to safeguard the complete anonymity of the call records while ensuring that any feed back we could provide to the operators could be made use of.

The data used in the trial are GSM toll tickets in an ASPeCT-specific subset of the archived Eurobill format. This particular format contains 25 fields, among which the ASPeCT tools can isolate the particularly important ones for fraud detection: A- and B-numbers (call originator and call recipient subscriber numbers), the call starting time, the duration of the call.

We obtained a set of data containing approximately 4 months worth of toll tickets for approximately 20,000 users. The users were chosen as a series of CHARGED-IMSI groupings to capture an expected wide range of behaviours within the data. The toll tickets were collected and stored on a daily basis. Once collected, they were concatenated into approximately 100 files for distribution, training and processing. From this data it would also be possible to select a smaller subset of the users to further reduce the size of the data set.

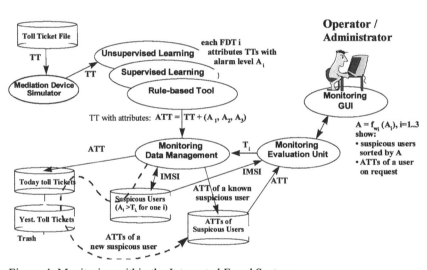

Figure 4: Monitoring within the Integrated Fraud System

All subscriber information contained in the respective toll ticket fields, and also all information that allows distinction between individual users, was encrypted whilst preserving the 25-field format. Thus, the confidentiality of personal data was protected while the case individuality is retained. Any suspicious users that are identified can be investigated by the operators by reversing the *sanitization* process.

The trial system was that shown in Figure 3 and Figure 4.

A billing mediator is simulated to give the effect of the near-real-time arrival of toll tickets collected from all operators.

User profiles must be swapped between disk and main memory each time a new toll ticket arrives at the fraud detection tool. The performance requirements are severe, as peak performance must exceed 30 toll tickets per second. We obtain such performance by using a simple, but optimised database tool called GDBM. The database is accessed by a key, which is the IMSI of the user and provides a content which is the concatenation of the Current User Profile and User Profile History.

Combination of the different tools

The common alarm level $A_{com} = f(w_1, w_2, w_3, A_1, A_2, A_3)$ will be used for the ordering. The function f is used for combining the thresholds computed by all tools to a common alarm level. The weights w_i will allow users manually to adjust the influence of each tool on the common result. One of the main tasks of the trial was to determine a well-suited function on combining the results.

We opted for a well-known approach from statistical theory: logistic regression modelling. The combination function has then the form $f = 1/(1+\exp(-\Sigma \, w_i A_i))$. The advantages of this combination function are the following:

a. The determination of the parameters w_i is straightforward. The necessary optimisation can be based fully on the individual results of the different tools (B-number analysis, unsupervised neural network, supervised neural network, and rule-based system) on a training-set similar to the one used in the development of the supervised neural network

b. The number of parameters that have to be estimated is low and the optimisation procedure is guaranteed to converge to an optimal solution.

c. The resulting parameters w_i are also statistically meaningful in that contributions with large parameter values contribute exponentially more to the probability of fraud than contributions with low parameter values. This interpretation means that our integrated tool is building an estimate of the probability of fraud on the basis of the behaviour of a user.

This logistic regression modelling provides a start estimate of the relative weighting of the individual tools. Adjusting the weights during the daily operation of the fraud detection engine will be a task of an administrator. The same holds for changing the thresholds for a minimum suspicion. An adjustable global threshold T_{com} will allow the raising of an alarm, if A_{com} exceeds T_{com}. This is meant for the critical cases where the tool should alert an operator and in a later stage could propose responsive countermeasures. In our software implementation of the fraud detection tool, the operator uses a simple web browser interface to adapt these weights manually.

From the three million or so toll tickets processed 27 possible fraudsters were identified. Further analysis was able to clear all but 4 of these from operational data (mainly hire phones, changes of SIM - identity module - in the phone, and unbarring of international calling). The four were to be pursued by the operators.

This performance was seen as encouraging by the operators. The ratio of false positives to true positives was good. Given the greatly reduced incidence of fraud resulting from GSM, the tool would be effective in identifying a significant portion of the remanent abuse.

5   Legal considerations

5.1   Legal background

An extensive study was conducted by ICRI[a] in the context and from the perspective of the ASPeCT project. It has, as its objective, the determination of the legal rules applying in the various fields of law affected by the use of fraud detection systems by mobile communications operators or service providers.

Mobile telecommunications operators use call data records for fraud detection purposes. They contain details relating to every mobile phone call attempt. Toll tickets are transmitted to the network operator by the cells or switches that the mobile phone was communicating with. They are used to determine the charge to the subscriber, but they also provide information about customer usage and thus four legal questions were examined with regard to the use of fraud detection systems:

1. Do operators monitoring calls on the network for fraud detection purposes, act against the fundamental principle of the *confidentiality* of private telecommunications? The confidential character is not limited to the content of the calls but extended to all kinds of data with regard to the call, such as the identity and location of the calling and the called parties, the time and the duration of the call, etc.
2. Are operators processing call data for fraud detection purposes, *controllers* of the processing of personal data in the legal sense? If so, what are the consequences of the application of personal *data protection* rules? Which law will be applicable to the processing of call data, when more than one country is involved as is often the case in the context of mobile communications[b]?
3. Given the fact that the results of the fraud detection system are always computer-readable data, how has this data to be presented as *evidence* in court? Will the courts in the E.U. Member States accept the data resulting from fraud detection systems as admissible evidence?

---

[a] Interdisciplinair Centrum voor Recht en Informatica - Interdisciplinary Centre for Law and Information Technology – K. U. Leuven, <http://www.law.kuleuven.ac.be/icri/>
[b] This is particularly difficult to resolve: consider user *a* subscribing to network *N* in country *A* travelling (roaming) in country *X* calling user *b* subscribing to network *M* in country *B* travelling (roaming) in country *Y*; *who has legal jurisdiction?*

4. If the data resulting from the fraud detection system is accepted and there is no doubt that fraud has been committed, how will the different fraud types identified in mobile telecommunications be legally qualified? Is telecommunications fraud considered as a specific type of crime or do we have to use general qualifications such as theft, deception, forgery, conspiracy to defraud etc.

Each of these questions was dealt with in a separate chapter of the full report[4].

Telecommunications privacy

As far as the issue of telecommunications privacy is concerned, there seem to be three types of national legislation with regard to the possibility for network operators or service providers to process call data concerning their subscribers.

A first type of legislation does not explicitly grant an exception to network operators or service providers to process call data but accepts such practices implicitly.

A second type of legislation explicitly grants an exception to network operators to register call data as far as this is necessary for the proper functioning of the network or the provision of the telecommunications service.

A third type of legislation explicitly grants an exception to network operators or service providers to register call data for fraud detection purposes but may submit this exception to specific conditions.

Data protection

It is evident that the data protection laws of the E.U. Member States, enacted over a period of more than twenty years, contain a wide variety of solutions. It is precisely on this point that the European Commission took the initiative to propose a Directive in this field. This Directive – 95/46/EC – was enacted on 24 October 1995. All Member States of the E.U. were required to transpose the provisions of this Directive in their national law.

At this time, all the Member States are changing their data protection law in order to make it compatible with the provisions of the Directive.

An essential principle of the Directive is the so-called *finality principle* stating that personal data collected for a certain purpose (billing, for example) should not be used for other – secondary – purposes, unless certain conditions have been fulfilled. One of the conditions is the duty to inform the data subject about the secondary use.

The Directive also contains very specific rules about the question of which law has to be applied when personal data are processed in more than one Member State. The criterion set forward by the Directive is the "establishment of the controller". Export of personal data outside the European Union is forbidden to countries without an "adequate level" of personal data protection.

Electronic data as evidence

Electronic data is adducible as evidence in all the EU Member States. Legislation enacted in 1984 (UK) and 1992 (Ireland) ensure the admissibility of such evidence in the common law jurisdictions while the principle of free proof is used in the civil law jurisdictions to guarantee the admissibility of data as evidence. In addition, civil law courts sometimes have a broad discretion regarding what they will accept as evidence.

Legal qualification of electronic fraud

The study examines the issue of how one legally qualifies various types of mobile telecommunications fraud. Does the law of the E.U. Member States contain a legal qualification of telecommunications fraud as a specific incrimination? Is there a specific criminal treatment of telecommunications fraud? Or do we have to fall back on traditional criminal categories?

The task of qualifying different types of cellular fraud does not fit neatly into one particular field of law. In addition to qualifying the different types of cellular fraud, the report also contains the relevant legislation used to prosecute cellular fraud and the possible legal remedies available to counteract mobile fraud in the relevant member states.

5.2 Telecommunications privacy

A mobile communications network operator planning to register call data for fraud detection purposes has to take into account the legal rules concerning the protection of telecommunications privacy.

The starting principle of these rules is the confidential nature of all private communications. The confidentiality does not only include the content of the calls but also concerns all other data relating to the calls such as the identity of the correspondents, their location, the time and the duration of the call, etc.

The question is therefore the following: *can the rules with regard to the confidentiality of private telecommunications constitute an obstacle for the processing of call data for fraud detection purposes?*

The right of the individuals to keep their communications confidential is recognised at international level, in the European Convention for the Protection of Human Rights and Fundamental Freedoms[a] and in the recently adopted European directive concerning the processing of personal data and the protection of privacy in the telecommunications sector[5].

Also the national laws of the Member States, and sometimes even the Constitutions, contain provisions protecting the confidentiality of communications.

---

[a] This Convention was signed in Rome on the 4th of November 1950, in the framework of the Council of Europe.

These rules are however not absolute and often exceptions are provided by the national laws in order to allow police, courts or other authorities to circumvent the privacy of communications but with appropriate legal safeguards and sanctions.

The study analysed the national rules regarding confidentiality of telecommunications and the exceptions to these rules The aim was to evaluate any possible legal problems which network operators can face when putting into practice fraud-detection systems in the field of mobile communications.

European legislation

The ASPeCT project made a comprehensive survey of existing Member State law which is beyond the scope of this chapter, but we include here the principal items of European legislation.

Article 8 of the European Convention of Human Rights

It is recognised at the international level that everyone has the right to respect for his private and family life, his home and his correspondence, as it is stated in article 8 of the European Convention for the Protection of Human Rights and Fundamental Freedoms.

However, this article of the European Convention of Human Rights (ECHR) allows certain exceptions to this rule when the following conditions are fulfilled:

any interference with this right should be in accordance with the law: this means that the network operator can only take fraud prevention measures which interfere in one way or another with the privacy rights of the mobile telephone users if this interference is regulated by a law.
the interference should be necessary in a democratic society in the interests of national security, public safety or the economic well-being of the country, for the prevention of disorder of crime, for the protection of heath or morals or for the protection of rights and freedoms of others.

The European Court of Human Rights has clarified somewhat the scope of these conditions in the framework of the Malone case[6], in which the applicant alleged violation of article 8 of the ECHM under two heads:

Interception of his postal and telephone communications by or on behalf of the police;
"Metering" of his telephone by or on behalf of the police.

Regarding the first condition, the Court made it clear that the expression "in accordance with the law" should be interpreted in the light of the general principles as stated in the Sunday Times judgement of 26 April 1979[7] to apply to the comparable expression "prescribed by law":

The word "law" is to be interpreted as covering not only written law but also unwritten law.

The interference in question must have a basis in domestic law.

Both expressions were however also taken to include requirements over and above compliance with domestic law. Two of these requirements are the following:

The law must be adequately accessible;
A norm can not be regarded as law unless it is formulated with sufficient precision to enable the citizen to regulate his conduct[8]

The Court also reiterated its opinion that the phrase "in accordance with the law" does not merely refer back to domestic law but also relates to the quality of the law, requiring it to be compatible with the rule of law, which is expressly mentioned in the preamble to the Convention.

It appears at first sight that the second condition imposed by article 8.2 of the ECHR will be less difficult to satisfy since it is clear that the measures which a network operator might wish to put into practice to prevent fraud are motivated by the need for preventing a disorder or crime: fraud.

However, it should also be taken into account that the European Court of Human Rights specified, in the Malone case above, that an interference can only be regarded as "necessary in a democratic society" if the particular system of secret surveillance adopted contains adequate guarantees against abuse.

The essential rule to be deduced from the analysis of article 8 of the European Convention of Human Rights is that any exception to the principle of the confidential nature of private communications has to be based on a law. The conclusion is that a network operator or service provider is not allowed to process call data for fraud detection purposes unless a law permits him to do so.

Article 5 of the European Telecommunications Privacy Directive

After more than seven years of negotiations, the European telecommunications directive was formally approved by the Telecommunications Council on the 1st of December 1997 and published in the Official Journal of 30 January 1998. This directive bears the date of 15th December 1997.

The aim of this directive is to apply for the specific purposes of telecommunications networks the general data protection principles laid down in Directive 95/46/EC[9]. It is designed, in a constantly changing field, to prevent Member States' legislation from developing along different lines in ways which may jeopardise the single market in telecommunications services and terminal equipment, but at the same time ensuring a high level of protection for the rights of individuals, in particular, their right to privacy.

This directive emphasises the increasing risk associated with automated storage and processing of data relating to subscribers and users[a].

The European telecommunications privacy directive can have important consequences for the ASPeCT project's results since it regulates the type of information that telecommunications operators may collect on their customers and

---

[a] See recital n. 6 of the preamble to this directive.

extends protection to subscribers who are natural and legal persons. According to this directive, traffic data collected by telecommunications operators must, in principle, be erased or made anonymous at the end of the call.

It will be necessary to take into account the provisions of this directive, together with the ones of the general data protection directive of 1995[10], at the moment of building security tools for the detection of fraud in mobile telecommunications.

The telecommunications privacy directive contains specific provisions dealing with security and confidentiality of the communications, processing of traffic and billing data, itemised billing, presentation and restriction of calling and connected line identification, automatic call forwarding, directories of subscribers, unsolicited calls, technical features and standardisation.

In particular, article 6 of the draft directive, which refers to traffic and billing data, can play a fundamental role in the ASPeCT context since it specifically refers to the use of these data for purposes of fraud detection and makes this use subject to certain conditions.

The most important article of this directive when dealing with telecommunications privacy is article 5, which is dedicated to the confidentiality of the communications.

This article reads as follows:

1. *Member States shall ensure via national regulations the confidentiality of communications by means of public telecommunications network and publicly available telecommunications services. In particular, they shall prohibit listening, tapping, storage or other kinds of interception or surveillance of communications, by others than users, without the consent of the users concerned, except when legally authorised, in accordance with Article 14(1).*
2. *Paragraph 1 shall not affect any legally authorised recording of communications in the course of lawful business practice for the purpose of providing evidence of a commercial transaction or of any other business communication.*

The content of article 5 of the European telecommunications privacy directive is actually very similar to the article 8 of the European Convention of Human Rights. In practice, it brings us to exactly the same conclusion: the confidentiality of communications should be respected as a general principle but certain exceptions are allowed when they are authorised by law.

In other words, the solution will have to be found by examining the national legislation of the Member States.

The deadline for implementation of this directive was October 1998, with a two-year extension for the provisions in confidentiality of telecommunications (article 5 of this directive).

5.3   Personal data protection

Fraud detection is essentially based on the analysis of call data. From a legal point of view call data have to be considered as "personal data" falling under the scope of the personal data protection legislation. Personal data is, indeed, all kinds of data relating to a natural person who is, or can be, identified.

Processing of individual call data is unlawful if the provisions of the national data protection laws are not respected. Basic principles such as the right of the individual to be kept informed of the purposes for which data concerning him are being processed, or to have a right of access to the personal data which concern him/her, have therefore to be taken into account.

Why is a correct application of personal data protection legislation so vital in case of mobile communications fraud detection?

The reason is that evidence collected in an unlawful manner, for instance using methods contrary to the principles of personal data protection, will not be accepted in court proceedings.

Convention 108 of the Council of Europe
Successful discussions with the aim of preparing a European Convention in this domain took place in the Council of Europe and led to the approval of Convention 108 for the protection of individuals with regard to automatic processing of personal data. It was opened for signature on 28 January 1981. Convention 108 is an important legal instrument in the data protection field, not only because of the early date in which it was enacted but also because of the generality of the principles, which are set out in a manner which allows adaptation to evolving situations[11].

The purpose of the Convention, as stated on its article 1, is "to secure in the territory of each Party for every individual, respect for his rights and fundamental freedoms, and, in particular, his right to privacy, with regard to automatic processing of personal data relating to him". Data protection is considered a fundamental human right, intimately linked to the right of privacy (article 8 of the European Convention on Human Rights and Fundamental Freedoms).

The key-idea on which the Convention is based is that uniform principles for privacy protection which are applicable throughout different States provide a legal safety net for individuals and help to resolve international conflicts[12]. The Convention is, however, of a non-self-executing character, which in practice means that individuals may not directly invoke the Convention before their national Courts. The Convention holds mainly obligations for the States themselves. The principal obligation for them, resulting from the Convention, is the obligation to enact a national data protection law. The existence of such a law is a prerequisite for the ratification of the Convention.

Article 12 deals with trans-border flows of personal data. The aim of this article is to reconcile the requirements of effective data protection with the principle of free flow of information, regardless of frontiers, enshrined in article 10 of the European Convention for Human Rights[13]. This principle of free flow of personal data inside Europe could be very important in the area of mobile communications fraud detection.

The Convention has been ratified by all Member States of the European Union. The text of the Convention has also served as inspiration for most of the national data protection laws in Europe and recently also for the Directive 95/46/EC of the Council and the European Parliament, which will be the basic legal text in this domain in Europe for the forthcoming years.

Present status

It is evident that the data protection laws of the E.U. Member States, enacted over a period of more than twenty years, contain a wide variety of solutions. In 1973, when the first law was enacted in Sweden, the IT landscape was dramatically different from the one in the nineties. Mainframe computing was still predominant and limited to large organisations. This explains for instance why the first laws still started from the belief that individuals could be protected ideally by requiring a state license for every single processing of personal data. For the legislator acting in 1992, when personal computing had conquered the world, such a licensing regime did not seem practicable.

Because the Convention 108 of the Council of Europe was formulated using very general wording, it permitted a number of different interpretations. It is precisely on this point that the European Commission took the initiative to propose a draft Directive in this field. This Directive – 95/46/EC – was enacted on 24 October 1995. All Member States of the E.U. were required to transpose the provisions of this Directive in their national law by 24 October 1998.

All the Member States are currently changing their data protection law in order to make it compatible with the provisions of the European Directive.

The European Data Protection Directive: free flow of personal data

The European Directive is based on the fact that differences in the level of protection of the rights and freedoms of individuals, notably the right to privacy, with regard to the processing of personal data afforded in the Member States may prevent the transmission of such data from the territory of one Member State to that of another. This difference may therefore constitute an obstacle to the pursuit of a number of economic activities at Community level, distort competition and impede authorities in the discharge of their responsibilities under Community law.

Art. 1.2 of the Directive clearly and unambiguously establishes the basic principle that within the EU, there shall be no prohibitions or restrictions in the free flow of personal data between the Member States for reasons connected with the protection of the right of privacy. This text is substantially different from that in the Council of Europe Convention 108 under which it was possible for a Member State to forbid the export of data to EC countries with a low level of protection.

The Directive thereby fulfils one of its two basic aims, to ensure such free transfer of data within the European Union, considered as vital for the functioning of the Single Market, which will not be anymore restricted by the existence of different national laws with different provisions regarding the trans-border flows of information. Differing requirements originated at national level naturally affect the overall design and operation of any intended international network or database arrangement[14].

As far as non-EC countries are concerned, the transmission of personal data is restricted if the country in question lacks an adequate level of data protection (article 25). The adequacy of the level of protection afforded by a third country must be interpreted in such a way as to ensure that privacy of the citizens is not endangered by the export. It shall be assessed in the light of all the circumstances surrounding a data transfer operation or set of transfer operations.

The text of the Directive attaches special importance to the existence of an independent supervisory authority in each Member State which is seen as an essential component of the protection of individuals with regard to the processing of personal data and to which very relevant functions should be entrusted.

Scope of the Directive

The scope of application of the data protection Directive is defined in its article 3, saying that it will apply to the processing of personal data wholly or partly by automatic means and to the processing otherwise than by automatic means of personal data which form part of a filing system or are intended to form part of a filing system. Two elements need therefore to be defined: personal data and processing.

5.4　Admissibility of electronic evidence

Introduction

The third aspect of the study covered the issues of whether electronic data is admissible as evidence in the courts of selected Member States[a] of the EU and in which forms such evidence may be adduced in courts. Important issues such as relevant legislation, general court practice and requirements concerning witnesses are covered in the full report.

Objective

The need for our study results from the fact that mobile telecommunications operators use call data records (toll tickets) for fraud detection purposes. They contain details relating to every mobile phone call attempt. Toll tickets are transmitted to the network operator by the cells or switches that the mobile phone was communicating with. They are used to determine the charge to the subscriber, but they also provide information about customer usage and thus facilitate the detection of any possible fraudulent use. Such data would be relied on as evidence where a case is brought against a suspected fraudulent user.

Call data, being electronic in nature, differs from the usual paper-based evidence submitted in court. This raises two questions: Firstly, is electronic evidence adducible in domestic courts in the E.U. and secondly, if so, in what form should it be presented.

Generally speaking, electronic data is admissible as evidence in all EU Member States. Specific legislation allows for this in the EU's two common law jurisdictions, namely Ireland and the UK (except for Scotland, which has a civil law system) while the EU's civil law jurisdictions permit this type of evidence under their general freedom of proof principle. While electronic data is admissible as evidence in domestic courts, it should also be borne in mind that the legal profession is conservative by nature and certain members of the judiciary may not feel entirely comfortable dealing with this type of evidence. Another factor to consider is the disparities that exist between Member States in terms of how much they have embraced the IT revolution. Attitudinal differences become reflected in IT facilities in courtrooms and in the approach of judges.

Naturally, the rules of evidence differ from Member State to Member State. This is also true of the rules of court regulating the format in which such evidence must be adduced at trial.

The aim was to paint a clear picture of the evidential situation prevailing in the Member States covered by this chapter. This will be beneficial for mobile operators as they will be able to determine, using our information, the relevant legislation or legal principle governing the area of cellular fraud in the Member State concerned. It also helps establish the differences and similarities that exist between Member States when it comes to admitting electronic data as evidence.

Conclusion

Electronic data is adducible as evidence in all the EU Member States covered by the study. Legislation enacted in 1984 (UK) and 1992 (Ireland) ensure the admissibility of such evidence in the common law jurisdictions covered here while the principle of free proof is used in the civil law jurisdictions to guarantee the admissibility of data as evidence. In addition, civil law courts sometimes have a broad discretion regarding what they will accept as evidence.

Legal qualification of mobile communications fraud

The study examined the issue of how one legally qualifies various types of mobile telecommunications fraud. Does the law of the E.U. Member States contain a legal qualification of "telecommunications fraud" as a specific incrimination? Is there a specific criminal treatment of telecommunications fraud? Or do we have to fall back on traditional categorizations?

The task of qualifying different types of cellular fraud does not fit neatly into one particular field of law. In addition to qualifying the different types of cellular fraud, the study covered the relevant legislation used to prosecute cellular fraud and the possible legal remedies available to counteract mobile fraud in the respective Member States.

To tackle the question of the legal qualification of mobile telecommunications fraud, the twelve fraud types identified above were used.

The response to the ICRI survey of Member State legal positions is given fully in the report. Although the results cannot be viewed as a completely comprehensive picture, there emerges an indication that there is legislation addressing all twelve of our fraud types in several Member States. Ireland and The Netherlands reported some appropriate law for every case, however the picture may be slightly skewed by the diligence of the national correspondents – or the moral pressure exerted on them by their ICRI colleagues

6   Conclusions

The project produced a number of technical achievements, which may individually or collectively be taken up commercially to combat what will continue to be a significant threat to the revenues of the mobile industry as well as being a threat to the operational well-being of a service on which we are becoming increasingly dependent. These are:

Refinement of state-of-the-art AI techniques to address the specific problem of fraud detection.
Incorporation of an unsupervised behaviour profiling component.
Successful implementation and demonstration of individual tools, discovering their relative strengths at detecting aberrant activity in a communications network .
Subsequent integration of the tools to combine the strengths of the individual components.
Performance such as to be easily scaleable to the on-line handling of toll tickets in near real time.
Trials successfully identifying a number of previously undetected suspicious subscribers.
Flexible JAVA-based GUI and modular environment to facilitate development of a commercial product.
Analysis of the current legal situation and constraints which provides a basis for future rationalisation of law and guidance to current operators and services providers.

There have been early expressions of interest in commercial development of our results into fraud detection products. There is further scope for the techniques in the surveillance and management of other complex systems, notably behaviour of communications networks. Even further afield, one of the academic partners is providing consultancy on the applicability of the techniques we developed to the processing of medical diagnostic data.

The legal survey undertaken by the project has provided a comprehensive view of the state of existing legal response to the pursuit of mobile fraud and provides essential guidance to the industry concerning its plans for detection tools and countermeasures.

References

1. J. Shawe-Taylor, K. Howker and P. Burge. *Detection of Fraud in Mobile Telecommunications* Elsevier Information Security Technical Report, Vol. 4 No.1 ed. Z. Ciechanowicz .

2. URL: http://www.esat.kuleuven.ac.be/cosic/aspect/: ASPeCT Publicly available documents, (D18) Fraud Detection Concepts: Final Report, edited by P. Gosset

3. URL: http://www.esat.kuleuven.ac.be/cosic/aspect/: (D20) Project final report and results of trials

4. URL: http://www.esat.kuleuven.ac.be/cosic/aspect/: (D25) Legal aspects of fraud detection; J. Dumortier, M. Hyland, D. Alonso Blas

5. OJ .1998. L 24, Volume 41, of 30 January, p.1; *Directive 97/66/EC of the European Parliament and the Council of 15 December 1997* (concerning the processing of personal data and the protection of privacy in the tele-communications sector)

6. Malone judgement of 2 August 1984, Publ. Court, Series A, vol. 82, p. 30 and following.

7. Publ. Court, Series A, no. 30

8. Sunday Times judgement, p. 31, § 49; Silver and other judgement, p. 33, §§ 87 and 88

9. D. Alonso Blas. 1998. The implications of the new European privacy directive on telecommunications. *In Proceedings of the 9th ACTS Concertation Plenary and Domain Meetings*, 17-18 February 1998, ACTS, European Commission, DG XIII, Directorate B, 213-216.

10. OJ L 281, 23.11.95, p.31.*European directive 95/46/EC of the European Parliament and the Council of 24 October 1995* (on the protection of individuals with regard to the processing of personal data and on the free movement of such data)

11. Council of Europe. 1989. *New technologies: a challenge to privacy protection?* Study prepared by the Committee of experts on data protection under the authority of the European Community on Legal Co-operation, Strasbourg.

12. M.D. Rostoker and R.H. Rines. 1986. Chapter VII in *Computer jurisprudence: legal responses to the information revolution.* (USA: Oceana publications, INC)

13. Explanatory chapter on the Convention for the protection of individuals with regard to automatic processing of personal data, Convention opened for signature on 28 January 1981, Strasbourg 1981.

14. C. Hoyle. 1992. Trans-border data flows: many barriers stand in the way for users. *The International Computer Lawyer*, **1**(1).

Chapter 9

Detecting Payment Card Fraud with Neural Networks

Khosrow Hassibi
Director of Fraud Solutions Core Technology,
HNC Software Inc.

1 Fraud is a rare but costly event

Despite the large amount of money lost to credit card fraud in recent years, it is actually a fairly rare event. Out of some 12 billion transactions made annually, approximately 10 million—or one out of every 1200 transactions— turn out to be fraudulent. Also, 0.04% (4 out of every 10,000) of all monthly active accounts are fraudulent. Today's fraud detection systems are designed to prevent a mere one-twelfth of one percent of all transactions processed.

In the financial industry, annual fraud losses are calculated using a measurement called fraud basis points. Currently, U.S. fraud losses amount to lower than 10 fraud basis points[a] (0.10%). This means that out of every one dollar, one tenth of a cent is lost to fraud. In the U.S., fraud basis points have consistently decreased in the last few years due to sophisticated fraud detection tools and improvements in fraud operation/prevention.

As one can see in Figure 1A, annual Visa/MasterCard International (MCI) credit card fraud losses from 1988 to 1998 amounted to approximately 750 million dollars[b] in the United States. This is a very small portion of the total credit card charge volume of almost 750 billion dollars for the same year represented in Figure 1B. Because a subset of fraud cases always go undetected, unreported, or

---

[a] Other sources indicate a fraud basis point anywhere between 8 to 10.
[b] It is not clear whether these numbers are net fraud charge-offs after recoveries or simply gross numbers. American Express and Discover Financial Services Inc. do not disclose fraud numbers but have experienced similar trends.

misreported, actual fraud losses are probably higher than what the industry tends to report.

Note that after growing at a rapid rate between 1989 and 1992, total yearly fraud losses have stayed somewhat flat since1993. During the same period, the total charge volume on Visa/MCI cards in the U.S. more than doubled from 350 Billion dollars to more than 750 Billion dollars. The number of cards issued in U.S. also doubled in this period. As one can see in Figures 1C and 1D, number of cards and charge volume worldwide have significantly increased in this period too. From 1989 to 1992, credit card fraud losses were rapidly growing at least in direct proportion to the card volume increase and usage (15-20% growth rate).

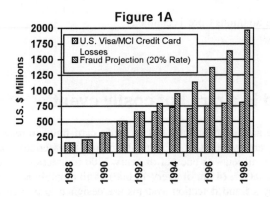

Figure 1A

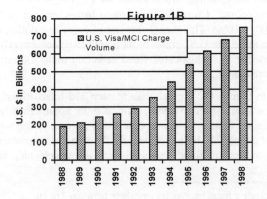

Figure 1B

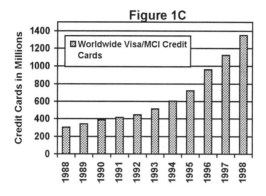

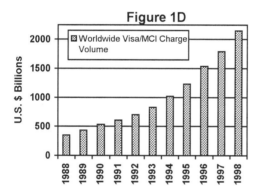

Figure 1: Statistics on U.S. and worldwide Visa/MCI credit cards[1].

2 Bringing fraud losses under control with Falcon

In 1992, new fraud detection initiatives including FalconTM, HNC's patented neural network payment card fraud detection system, helped to significantly reduce fraud losses in the U.S. We used a 20% fraud loss growth rate in Figure 1A to illustrate what the losses would have been if the trend had continued.

Since its launch in 1992, Falcon has enjoyed tremendous international success as a complete fraud detection system. Currently, forty out of the top fifty Visa/MasterCard issuers use Falcon in the United States, the most mature payment card market in the world. And in recent years, Falcon installations have also increased in major countries on all five continents. Today, sixteen out of the top twenty-five Visa/MasterCard issuers worldwide use Falcon. Figure 2 shows worldwide Falcon growth since 1992. The vertical axis indicates the total number of payment cards under Falcon protection during last 8 years.

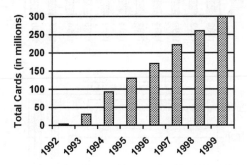

Figure 2: Worldwide Falcon growth since its inception in 1992

The rare occurrence of fraud transactions makes detecting them a very challenging technical problem. Prior to Falcon, issuers had to rely on cumbersome paper reports and trained human experts to detect fraud. By the time a fraudulent transaction was identified using these methods, it was usually too late to avoid a financial loss. Clearly, just keeping up with the shear volume of transactions was a challenge, as was the fact that fraud transactions can look deceptively like legitimate ones. For virtually every fraudulent charge, there are valid reasons why an honest cardholder would make exactly the same charge.

2.1   Falcon technology

Falcon uses Artificial Neural Networks (ANNs) to power its core decision engine. Before we developed Falcon, HNC successfully applied ANNs to solve a variety of difficult real-world problems, including hand print character recognition, a technology that is still widely used in handwritten check and form processing applications today.

In technical circles, Falcon is widely regarded as one of the most successful commercial applications of neural networks in the financial industry. Faced with vast quantities of valid transaction data in which fraudulent transactions are all too easily concealed, no fraud detection system can flag a transaction as fraudulent with 100% certainty (unless it is a very obvious fraud case, usually a rare and temporary occurrence). But a predictive model must provide a measure of certainty that a particular transaction is fraudulent. To accomplish this, HNC scientists and engineers use the latest techniques from Machine Learning, Adaptive Pattern Recognition, Neural Networks, and Statistical Modeling to develop Falcon predictive models. Due to their high performance, these predictive models have provided the industry with the best cost/benefit equation for fraud detection since 1992.

2.2 Falcon consortium data

In addition to its unique technology, another major strength of Falcon is its access to a huge base of payment card data. As part of their contract, most Falcon clients agree to provide payment card data with associated fraud tags to HNC on a continuous basis, usually monthly. Since Falcon has more than 80% of the payment card fraud detection market worldwide, this translates into a huge data pool. In the U.S. and most countries around the world, reducing payment card fraud is considered a benefit for all affected parties—issuers, cardholders, acquirers, merchants, and the economy as a whole. Therefore, most payment card issuers are usually eager to cooperate with each other in a non-competitive manner to reduce fraud by contributing data to the Falcon fraud consortium. The data pool is refreshed regularly and allows HNC to develop better, more robust models that benefit all fraud consortium members. For example, due to differences in fraud operations and maturity of fraud prevention tools among different issuers, the Falcon consortium data pool is less susceptible to severe data censoring. Also, fraud trends that may hit only a few issuers at first are captured in the consortium data before they have a chance to propagate to other members.

The Falcon fraud consortium provides issuers with a set of specifications for submitting their data. Each client must submit a variety of separate files, including authorization files, cardholder masterfiles, fraud files, payment files, non-monetary files, and posting files. A typical U.S. card issuer can authorize 1,000,000 transactions per day or more than 350 million authorizations per year. This data is captured in the authorization file. Given the fact that HNC has collected data from many leading issuers for the last several years, one gets an idea of the volume of data that is available to us. To manage this huge data pool, HNC has devised proprietary sampling techniques to generate train/test data sets.

3 Falcon system architecture

3.1 The Falcon decision engine

Figure 3 provides a high level view of the Falcon decision engine. Like any machine learning or pattern recognition system, it includes two main sub-systems: *Feature (variable) computation* and *Predictive model* (also known as *pattern recognizer* or simply *model*). The additional sub-system we call *Profiles* (or cardholder profiles) implements the *memory* for the system. From a dynamic system standpoint, profiles capture the *system states* for each cardholder. One can think of the whole predictive model as a dynamic system. Based on its inputs and states, the model outputs a score that indicates a measure of certainty for a current transaction being fraudulent. The individual components of the system depicted in Figure 3 are discussed in more detail in the following sections.

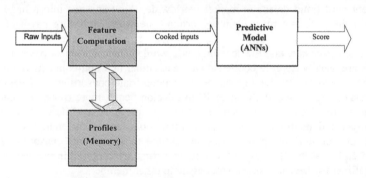

Figure 3: Falcon Decision Engine architecture

Raw inputs

The raw inputs for the decision engine come from many different sources in the payment card environment. They include data from authorization messages (ISO 8583)[2], posting transactions, cardholder master files, merchant information, and potentially non-monetary and payment transactions. Authorization information includes a variety of data pertaining to the current authorization in progress, such as account number, amount, date, time, merchant category code, and merchant zip code, to name just a few. Posting data —a list of all settled authorizations—is especially useful in environments that have a low authorization rate (less than 90%), typically in international set ups. On the issuer's side, cardholder data provides a variety of demographic information about the cardholder. This data includes the cardholder's location, age, account open date, and other information. Merchant data such as location, business category, and business name, are also used as raw inputs when available, along with payment and non-monetary transactions, such as address change, account inquiries, and new card requests.

Feature computation and cooked inputs

The most important function of any machine learning or pattern recognition system is computing the inputs that go into the predictive model. These are referred to as *cooked* or *transformed inputs*. The developer of the model should decide how to extract the most useful and powerful information from raw inputs, what transformations to use, and how to compute these inputs efficiently in real-time. Falcon uses a pool of several thousand cooked inputs[a]. These inputs are derived and extracted using a variety of proprietary transformations and computational schemes called filters. Simple examples of cooked inputs include a variety of statistics on the spending patterns of each cardholder, such as average amount spent for a particular category of products in short term, medium term, and long term ranges. HNC has gained extensive experience developing such variables for financial applications.

The Falcon score is not computed based solely on changes in individual cardholder spending patterns (behavior). Cardholders spending patterns change all the time due to lifestyle changes, season (holiday shopping, for example), and many other reasons. Therefore, a fraud detection system that relies exclusively on changes in spending patterns cannot provide an optimal false positive rate. To solve this problem, Falcon uses portfolio-wide fraud trends and fraud trend dynamics across a variety of sub-segments or clusters of the whole portfolio to compute a good portion of the cooked inputs. HNC scientists have developed proprietary feature computation techniques to capture variables from these clusters as well as variables from cardholder spending patterns. This combination of variables optimizes Falcon's performance.

Implementing memory with profiles

Further, the richness and variety of cooked inputs mandates the existence of memory, in a dynamic sense, for the Falcon predictive model. To achieve high performance, the predictive model needs to know about the historical spending patterns of each cardholder the system monitors. This means that each cardholder's spending patterns— at any point in time— must be available to the feature computation sub-system.

The feature computation sub-system uses both raw inputs and the stored information in profiles to generate cooked inputs. Profiles capture the past history of spending for each cardholder (cardholder behavior) in a compact and efficient format. Each profile is unique and personalized to a cardholder's past spending patterns. As a result, the model can generate the cooked inputs to make a decision based on the current and past transactions of each cardholder. The addition of

---

[a] Only a subset (tens to hundreds depending on the application) are usually used to build a model. A combination of proprietary and traditional variable selection techniques is used in this process.

profiles provides the system with both short and long term memory. As one can see, the design of profiles is very closely related to the design of cooked inputs.

Training the ANNs

Typically, Falcon predictive models use feed-forward ANNs trained on a variant of a back-propagation-training algorithm[3,4,5]. The ANNs collectively generate an output score based on cooked inputs, which in turn are computed based on raw inputs and profiles. The score is simply a number between 1 and 999 that measures the likelihood that a transaction is fraudulent. The higher the number, the greater the probability that the transaction is fraudulent.

HNC scientists use a variety of techniques to optimize model performance and to avoid over and under-training. Depending on the application, the training and test data sets usually contain tens of thousands to millions of exemplars For example, a consortium model —like those used in Falcon—usually requires larger train/test sets than a custom model. The consortium model data set must not only span the most recent credit card data submitted by consortium members, but should also include past data (one to a few years old) with proper de-emphasis. It's important to include past data to assure that the new predictive model will remember older fraud patterns— which may not be well represented in the most recent data— in case they return.

How the decision engine works in production

In a production environment, the Falcon decision engine receives raw data in a standard pre-specified format (called Falcon API, for Application Programming Interface). The feature computation sub-system computes all of the required cooked inputs in real-time based on the historical data preserved in the profiles. The sub-system updates the profiles based on the latest transaction data (raw inputs), and then sends the cooked inputs to the predictive model to generate a score. Note that the profiles for each and every cardholder are dynamically updated in production as soon as a transaction occurs. The predictive model, however, is static and is updated on a less frequent basis. For example, Falcon consortium models are reviewed quarterly and are usually updated only once a year. More frequent updates are unnecessary because the technology used by Falcon allows it to capture a more robust level of fraud dynamics, not just surface dynamics. As a result, even though some fraud trends may change at the surface, these changes will not affect Falcon's overall performance in between model updates. This is in contrast to other technologies, such as rule-based fraud detection systems, which only capture surface dynamics.

Other key system components

Although the decision engine acts as Falcon's brain, it is only a small part of the whole system. Installing Falcon in an issuer's authorization system requires integrating a variety of software and hardware components. Currently, Falcon is based on a client-server architecture that runs on a variety of platforms, including most Unix flavors and CICS. The system throughput can be as high as 120 tps (transactions per second), which is more than adequate for most applications. Figure 4 shows a high-level diagram of the four main hardware and software components of the Falcon system. Each component is described in more detail below.

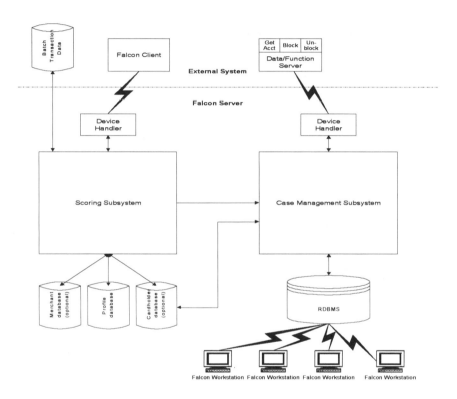

Figure 4: Falcon fraud detection system client-server architecture

Scoring subsystem: This subsystem interfaces with external authorization systems through a device handler. The interface provides the necessary communication to get raw inputs (required for scoring) and a variety of other data to the Falcon server. It is comprised of the Falcon decision engine and various processes for routing, monitoring, and scoring the raw data. The scoring subsystem also interfaces to a variety of databases, the most important being the Falcon cardholder profile database.

Scoring Engine Databases: The profiles are stored in the cardholder profile database. This is an indexed file that is designed for fast access. Any cardholder profile can be accessed with a maximum of two disk reads: one for the index and one for actual profile read. The two other databases for cardholder and merchant are optional. They are implemented if cardholder and merchant data is not directly available to the scoring server from the external system.

Case Management Subsystem: The main purpose of the Falcon score is to rank order accounts based on fraud risk. The optimal strategy is then to maximize frauds detected per customer contact by investigating the riskiest accounts first. The case management subsystem provides a work environment in which scored transactions can be ranked and presented to the analysts for investigation. Different queues can be created for working the flagged accounts. These include case reviews, assignment of the queues to analysts, and tracking a variety of performance measures, such as analyst performance. The case management system comprises a variety of processes for routing, spooling, and monitoring of the created cases. It uses traditional relational database management systems (Oracle, DB2, etc) to store all related information. Through a device handler, the case management system also interfaces to the external authorization system. Through this interface, it can perform a variety of tasks including accessing cardholder information from the external system and blocking/unblocking accounts.

Falcon Workstation: The analysts interact with Falcon through a client-side software running on standard PC hardware. The Falcon workstation provides different levels of security and login so that the access to the system can be controlled. For example, the queue definitions and assignments must only be accessible by the fraud operation manager and not the analysts. Fraud operations manager can access a variety of workflow and performance reports from Falcon workstations. The reports are created by the case management system and are stored in the RDBMS.

4   Measuring system performance

When using Falcon, an issuing bank sets a suspect threshold score. Transactions scoring above this threshold are either investigated further or referred outright. These transactions are either actual fraudulent transactions or legitimate transactions that appear suspect because they do not reflect a cardholder's usual spending patterns or they match known fraud patterns.

Account false-positive ratio versus score
To accurately assess a model's performance, an issuer must perform a type of cost-benefit analysis. The cost is proportional to the account false-positive ratio, or **AFPR**. The AFPR expresses the number of accounts identified incorrectly as fraudulent for each actual fraudulent account the model identifies. (For the purpose of model analysis, an account is identified as fraudulent if it has at least one transaction that scores above a "suspect threshold" score, although in practice a system such as Falcon may combine model scores with rules to generate fraud

cases.) The benefit is the number of correct fraud predictions the model makes. To compare the performance of one model to another, one looks for an increase in correct predictions and an AFPR that remains constant or declines. For instance, an AFPR of 10:1 indicates that for each genuinely fraudulent account that it finds, a model identifies 10 innocent accounts as fraudulent. The higher the threshold score, the more the AFPR goes down. However, by setting a higher threshold an issuer also identifies fewer actual frauds. Figure 5A shows the relationship between the Falcon score and AFPR.

Account detection rate and dollar detection rate versus score

HNC measures correct fraud prediction in two ways. The first is the account detection rate, or ADR. This is the number of correctly identified fraud accounts expressed as a percentage of all actual fraud accounts. For instance, if there are 1000 fraud accounts and the model correctly identifies 720 of them, then the ADR is 72 percent. Figure 5B shows the relationship between ADR and score. The second measure of correct fraud prediction is dollar detection rate, or DDR. This is the amount of money available to be saved (potential amount that could have been lost) on this and subsequent transactions, as the result of a correct fraud prediction. Therefore, DDR is a measure of *savings*. However, the savings are not computed with respect to the total left credit line potentially available to fraud (usually referred to as Open-To-Buy or OTB), but with respect to the amount actually lost to fraud based on historical data. The amount is expressed as a percentage of the total amount charged fraudulently against an account. For instance, if a fraudster attempts to charge $2,000 to an account in several transactions, and the model identifies the account as fraudulent in time to prevent $1,000 of those charges, then the DDR is 50 percent. DDR shows not merely whether a model catches fraud, but also how fast.

There are three measures of DDR, which depend on how an issuer's systems are set up to enable analysts to respond to fraud predictions:

Real-Time Mode: In real-time mode, the model produces a fraud score for a transaction before the transaction is completed. This enables the analyst to respond to the current transaction. Real-time mode permits the highest DDR.

On-Line Mode: In on-line mode, the model produces a fraud score for a transaction after it has been completed. This enables the analyst to respond to the transaction after the one for which the model has produced its most current score. On-line mode permits a somewhat lower DDR than real-time mode.

Batch Mode: In batch mode, transactions accumulate in a file, and batch files are sent periodically to the model for scoring. Typically, the model sees a new batch file and scores batch transactions once per day. Batch mode permits the lowest DDR.

The most advanced Falcon clients use a combination of real-time and on-line modes.

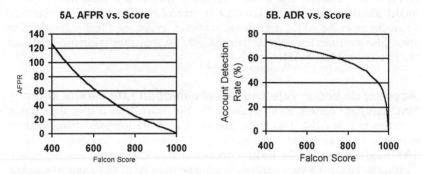

Figure 5: Typical relationship between AFPR and score (5A) and between ADR and score (5B)

Model performance versus AFPR

Neither ADR or AFPR on their own are sufficient to set an optimal operating point (a threshold) for the fraud detection system. However, by putting the two measures together, one can compute the overall cost-benefit of the system. It helps to think of ADR and DDR as measures of the overall benefit of the system, which is to stop frauds early and save money that could potentially be lost to fraud. On the other hand, one can think of AFPR as a measure of the cost of detecting fraud. We can collapse Figure 5A and 5B into one graph by simply eliminating the score (Figure 6A). The vertical axis (ADR or DDR) will be the benefit while the horizontal axis (AFPR) will be proportional to the cost of operating the system at any point.

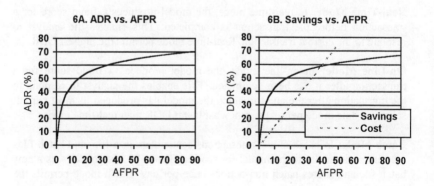

Figure 6: ADR and DDR versus (AFPR) in evaluating the benefit of a fraud detection system

Considering Figure 6A, the ADR at an AFPR of 20:1 is around 55%. This means the system detects 55% of all fraud accounts at a cost of flagging 20 non-fraud accounts for each fraud account detected. Considering that in the U.S., the account fraud rate is 2500:1 (computed based on monthly active), a 20:1 false positive with 55% detection is very significant.

Transaction-based measures

The account-based performance measures are very useful in helping clients assess Falcon model performance and have become de facto industry standards. However, HNC scientists and engineers use many other measures during model development to assess model performance. For example, one simple measure of score performance is the KS plot in which the developed system (intelligent system) performance is measured with respect to a system that rank orders the transactions randomly (a dumb system). Figure 7A shows the KS plot for a Falcon model. Note that this plot is transaction-based, meaning that the vertical (% fraud detected) and horizontal (% of total population) axes indicate percentages of transactions. Figure 7B, on the other hand, shows the Falcon score distribution curve for fraud and non-fraud transactions. As expected, Falcon scores fraud transactions much higher than non-fraud transactions, resulting in an optimal separation of the two given the fact that some frauds look like normal, non-fraudulent transactions and vice-versa.

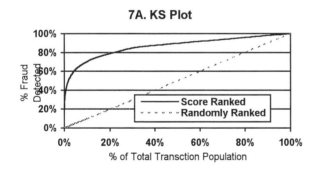

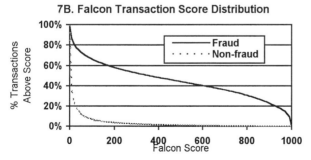

Figure 7: Sample transaction-based KS plot and score distribution for Falcon

Note: All charts depicted in this section are examples of a single Falcon model and are intended solely to illustrate score performance concepts. Actual performances could be significantly different based on portfolio characteristics, in particular overall population fraud rate.

6   Operational and human issues

6.1   Using the Falcon score

Payment card fraud happens quickly. So to prevent fraud effectively, issuers must first detect it as quickly as possible, before a fraudster has a chance to incur high losses on an account. After a fraud is detected, it's equally important that it be investigated quickly. Falcon helps issuers detect fraud faster. But it's up to the issuers to ensure that their fraud operations group work fraud cases in a timely manner.

As indicated earlier, the Falcon score rank orders accounts by fraud risk. The higher the score, the greater the likelihood of fraud. A typical approach to using the Falcon score is to use two thresholds. Transactions that score above the first threshold are automatically referred at the point of sale (real-time use of Falcon score). These transactions should have an extremely high likelihood of fraud, so this threshold is set at a very high score, typically in the 900 score band. Transactions that score above the second threshold-usually between 500 and 800-are placed in a case management queue for further investigation.

The highest scoring accounts must always be reviewed first since they are most likely to be fraudulent. Consequently, the optimal fraud operation strategy for queued cases is to investigate the riskiest accounts first. This maximizes the number of frauds caught per customer contacted. Investigation should proceed down the list, through successively less risky accounts (lower scored accounts), and continue until the incremental cost of detecting the next fraud outweighs the expected fraud savings. Figure 6B shows how the optimal threshold for fraud investigations varies depending on the investigation process cost, and the expected fraud savings at each risk level. The x-axis shows the fraud detection system false positive rate. The y-axis shows the percentage of total dollars that can be saved (DDR). In Figure 6B, it is assumed that the cost is linearly dependent on the AFPR. The business decision on what threshold score is optimal is client specific and depends on many factors.

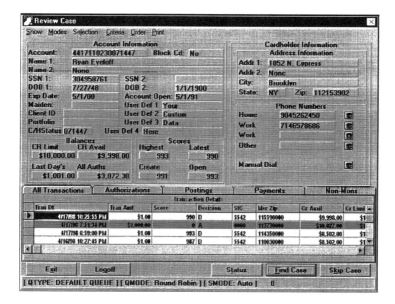

Figure 8: A Falcon Workstation Case Review screen as seen by an analyst

6.2 Human-computer interface

Like some other successful artificial intelligence systems, Falcon is not designed to replace a human, but to do things that humans are less well suited for. Falcon makes decisions very rapidly. It can make millions of quick decisions in a day without tiring or losing attention. In fact, its very specific and very long attention span is perhaps its greatest strength and least human-like characteristic. While Falcon is making millions of quick decisions based on the cardholder, transaction, and merchant information at its disposal, humans are left to do what they do best — communicating and investigating to stop the fraud.

Figure 8 shows a sample case review screen presented to Falcon analysts during review of a potential fraud account. The screen provides a variety of data for taking action and making decisions to the analysts. The data includes account information, such as name and account number, and cardholder data, such as most up to date address and phone numbers. The data also includes one click dialing, account balance information, the Falcon score, and detailed transaction history such as authorizations, postings, payments, and non-monetary transactions. Looking at the middle of screen, one can see the latest Falcon score on this account is 990 indicating a high fraud risk. The recommended procedure is to immediately try to contact cardholder to verify charges and to prevent potential losses prior to letting the analyst do any kind of investigation on the account[a]. This procedure is

---

[a] One should remember that fraud happens fast. Even a few minutes count here.

often referred to as "smile-and-dial." If the cardholder cannot be contacted immediately, then the best alternative is to let the analyst analyze the case. If the analyst concludes that the risk is very high, then he or she can perhaps temporarily block the account.

Although HNC has found the smile-and-dial approach to be the most effective, not all clients practice it. Some analysts simply do not want to rely on what the Falcon score suggests since the need for analysis and investigation—something most analysts like to perform—is significantly reduced. To prevent analyst burnout and attrition, some clients allow some level of analysis and investigation at the expense of more fraud losses.

Having the ability to write rules to detect fraud is often more personally rewarding for humans than simply relying on a score they may not understand. When HNC introduced *Falcon Expert*[TM], a rule-based system that supplements the Falcon scoring engine to catch flash frauds, it led to inefficiencies in some fraud shops. In these shops, fraud managers started writing rules that competed with the Falcon score rather than supplemented it. As a result, they lost focus and experienced higher fraud losses. HNC has worked with many clients to address these issues and to make recommendations for getting optimal use from the Falcon score in their operations while also being sensitive to the needs of their staff.

7   Comparing Falcon to other systems

When Falcon was originally introduced in 1993, it was a breakthrough system that provided the credit card issuers with a superior tool to combat fraud cost-effectively. The system's high up-front installation cost paid for itself in just a few months— even less for large issuers. Prior to the sudden surge in payment card fraud in the late 1980s and early 1990's, payment card fraud was simply regarded as a cost of doing business. During this period, issuers felt they could afford to rely on cumbersome paper reports and a handful of trained human experts to detect fraud, even though this approach offered limited success. While some issuers went so far as to write simple rules in their fraud authorization systems to decline or refer risky transactions, these rules were crude and also difficult to deploy and modify. In the early 1990s, an explosion in payment card fraud made it impossible for issuers to continue to ignore the problem. The need for more sophisticated fraud weapons provided the environment that gave birth to the more advanced fraud detection technologies available today.

Unfortunately, due to the commercial nature of fraud detection systems, there is no standard set of data, procedures, and tools for comparing them[a]. Consequently, HNC cannot make an apple-to-apple comparison of Falcon and other fraud detection systems. However, some of our clients have taken it upon themselves to

---

[a] Such standard data, procedures and tools exists for other commercial systems such as OCR (Optical Character Recognition). An independent organization conducts yearly tests on all candidate commercial OCR packages and publishes the results of the tests.

run "blind tests" of different candidate fraud detection systems before committing to one. In all the blind tests conducted by our clients, Falcon has out-performed the competition.

In laboratory simulations, HNC scientists and engineers have shown that by using ANNs in the Falcon decision engine, they can consistently get 30% to 100% better performance than traditional linear regression techniques, assuming both use the same Falcon cooked inputs. ANNs are so effective at detecting fraud because they can capture non-linear fraud patterns as well as interactions among various features (variables). Considering that a one-percentage point increase in fraud detection usually translates into savings of tens of thousand of dollars for a bank with a few thousand frauds per month, it's clear that ANNs make a significant contribution to Falcon's performance.

There are still a handful of issuers who rely on very complex rule-based systems comprised of as many as a thousand rules to detect fraud. While we do not know much about how well these systems perform compared to Falcon when it comes to detecting fraud, we do know that they are very costly and difficult to maintain. In comparison, we believe the Falcon neural network decision engine and models are easier to maintain and are more effective in fighting fraud.

In the last decade, the fight against fraud has proved to be one of the great success stories of the card industry. Faced with mounting fraud losses of more than 20 basis points in the early 1990s, sophisticated fraud detection and prevention technologies helped the card industry turn the problem around. Falcon has played a key role in this success. By complementing their existing fraud fighting strategies with neural network solutions like Falcon, issuers can make the most efficient use of their resources to keep fraud losses under control.

References

1. P. Demry. 1999. *Card Industry Directory*. (Faulkner & Gray, John Stewart, Publisher)

2. *Financial Transaction Card Originated Messages – Interchange Message Specifications: ISO 8583 Second Edition*. International Standards Organization (ISO), 1993-12-15.

3. D.E. Rumelhart, G.E. Hinton and R.J. Williams. 1986. Learning internal representations by error propagation in parallel distributed processing. In *Explorations in Microstructures of Cognition*, Vol. 1:Foundations (Cambridge, MA: MIT Press)

4. R. Hecht-Nielsen. 1990. *Neurocomputing* (Addison-Wesley)

5. T. Mitchell. 1997. *Machine Learning* (McGraw-Hill)

Chapter 10

Money Laundering Detection with a Neural-Network

Bernard Chartier and Thomas Spillane

Nestor, Inc.
One Richmond Square
Providence, RI 02906 USA
Tel: 401.331.9640
Fax: 401.331.7319
www.nestor.com

1   Introduction

Money laundering has become an increasingly proliferate crime perpetrated against, among other entities, financial institutions and investment firms worldwide. The magnitude of the problem and subtle nature of its infection of a financial institution dictate a non-trivial and more sophisticated detection solution than many of the rules-based systems being utilized today. In this article, Nestor, Inc., a leading worldwide provider of advanced money laundering detection solutions, presents a case study of the development and installation of a complete neural network-based money laundering solution that can be employed at large financial institution. The article discusses the development of the neural model – including data and related modeling issues – as well as a comparison of the system's detection rate relative to traditional rules-based detection systems. Additionally, the article describes the coupling of the neural network model with a user-friendly graphical user interface (GUI) and the integration of this comprehensive solution into the institution's existing production system, along with a number of practical production issues.

2   The scope of money laundering problem

Money laundering is defined as the process of transacting so as to convert illegally obtained funds to a form which appears to have originated from a legitimate source, thereby concealing the identity of the individuals who secured the funds[1]. The monies are never, even after laundering, legal, as legitimate appearance does not correspond to a legitimized state[2]. The magnitude of the problem worldwide is estimated at one trillion US dollars[3]. As the objective of laundering is concealment, and individual financial institutions have no incontrovertible source of data on funds laundered through their accounts, precise figures are difficult to obtain. Considering individual financial institutions, estimates of money laundered activity as a percent of total transaction activity are equally difficult to obtain, although informal figures obtained by Nestor range between 0-5% of all transactions, depending upon the size of the institution.

Laundering schemes that result in funds moving through financial institutions are varied and perpetually evolving, functions partly of the efforts of financial crimes enforcement entities. Most schemes involve three stages: placement, layering and integration[1]. In the placement phase, launderers alter the form of the monies, often depositing the funds as cash into an account. In the layering phase, multiple transactions are executed to disconnect the original monies from the launderer. In the final integration scheme, the launderer associates the money with an origin that appears legitimate, often a genuine or shell business. With schemes that involve financial institutions, transactions occur in all three laundering phases. This increases the likelihood of detection by a system which is sufficiently sophisticated to detect the subtle patterns of the scheme.

One simple example of a laundering scheme would be a large sum of drug money being deposited, placed, into a savings account, from which it is then transferred to a number of other accounts for layering purposes. Finally, it is moved into the account of a shell business, from which it is withdrawn as apparently legitimate cash. Most schemes are far more complex then this, and often involve multiple accounts, financial institutions and laundering vehicles.

Financial vehicles that can be involved in money laundering include, but are not limited to, savings, debit, credit and investment accounts. Launderers do not restrict their transaction activities to their own personal or business accounts, but also employ accounts of long-standing, previously legitimate individuals who allow the launderers to utilize their account for laundering purposes. These individuals are often compensated for the use of the account, but often do not actually perpetrate the laundering transactions themselves. This makes detection more challenging, as these accounts have a fusion of genuine and laundered transactions.

As with other risk management problems, the behavior of the target class of money launderers is similar, and in some cases inseparable, from that of genuine account holders. Consequently, in addition to presenting a low *a prior* incidence in the data, money-laundering detection is probabilistic. Further, neural network model features, which offer separation between the target classes, are both non-linear and non-Gaussian in distribution. Additionally, the feature space is a noisy one: neither the launderers or the genuine account holders conform to distinctive boundaries in the feature space, but present feature boundaries that are ill-defined and graduated.

3 Current methods of money laundering detection

Different countries have different laws regarding the monitoring and reporting of money movements. Most countries have a threshold value. Any amount above this threshold, including the full details of the transaction, must be reported to the appropriate government entity. Many countries also have laws that mandate the reporting of activity that is deemed suspicious by the financial institution, although some countries have far more liberal policies than others. As a result, launderers tend to target these countries more aggressively. Ethical and business considerations, along with these laws, drive financial institutions to attempt to identify money-laundering activity.

The quantified, precise nature of laws and transaction amount regulations lend themselves to implementation with a rules-based detection system. These systems allow risk managers to define precise rules that satisfy the laws and filter financial activity that may be suspicious. Figure 1 below depicts two rules mapped to a two-dimensional space. The vertical axis represents the number of deposits an account holder makes in a defined time period. The horizontal axis represents the maximum deposit amount fore these transactions. The rule in this case is:

If {(5 <= Number of Deposits 20) and (Deposit amount >= 10,000)}

Review account

Accounts that have any transactions at or above 10,000 units would be alerted, as would those with between two (2) and five (5) deposits in a defined period of time. Additional rules can be added, appearing as additional dimensions in the rules space, which would further isolate the laundered transactions. While such a rule may satisfy governmental regulations, its limitations are immediately apparent. For example, if a genuine account has five (5) deposits in the defined time period, it would be inappropriately alerted, appearing as a false positive. Conversely, if a money launderer has four (4) deposits in a particular time period, or has a one (1) 9,500-unit transaction, it would not be alerted. Furthermore, an expert familiar with money laundering must define the values of each rule boundary. This is an unappealing proposition for financial institutions that has not yet installed a detection system. Finally, these rules are static, and are not updated in an automated fashion, when money launderers or genuine account holders change their behaviors. Consequently, such a system in isolation would generate large numbers of false positives and false negatives.

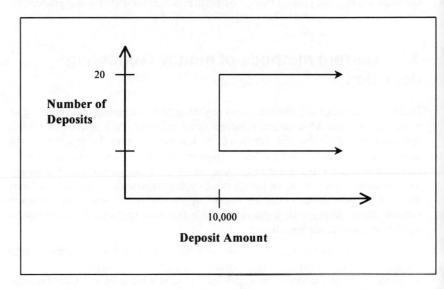

Figure 1: Two-dimensional depiction of a rule set defined to detect money laundered transactions

While a rigorous survey of the types of money laundering detection systems that financial institutions employ was not readily available at the time of publication of this article, an informal survey of the market place by the authors indicated that a significant number of institutions have either a rules-based system or no detection system at all. Given the limitations of such rules systems, it is clear that an artificially intelligent component must be added to maximize detection, minimize false positives and adapt to changing laundering and good trends in the portfolios.

4   Neural Network design

Given that money laundering is a low incidence, noisy and non-linear probabilistic pattern recognition problem, it lends itself well to resolution with a neural network. In addition to being an accurate pattern recognition engine, the neural algorithm should enable institutions to constantly update the neural network model, after it has been developed, with recent trends in laundering. This capability provides an ideal solution for money laundering that is known to be a dynamic problem.

To fulfill these requirements, Nestor employs its patented Probabilistic Restricted Coulomb Energy (PRCE) algorithm[4,5,6]. This algorithm is a radial basis function (RBF) type of neural network. Nestor incorporates a three-layer feed-forward architecture for all modeling. In general, an RBF network applies the values of the input vector to the input layer and establishes these as activation levels for neurons in the second, hidden layer. The hidden layer is comprised of perceptrons that are radius limited, and whose activation level is computed as follows:

$$y_j^2 = S(u_j) = S\left(\left(\sum_{j=1}^{M^1}\left(y_j^1 - \omega_{ij}^1\right)^2\right)^{1/2} - x_j\right) \tag{1}$$

where

- All superscripts denote the index of the layer
- ω^j indicates the synaptic weight between the jth and (j+1)th layers
- M^j indicates the number of cells in the jth layer
- $S(.)$ indicates a step function in which $S(u_j)$ is 0 for $u_{j>0}$ and $S(u_j) = 1$ for all $u_{j<0}$

The activation levels of the output layer are calculated according to the following:

$$y_i^3 = O(u_i) = O\left(\sum_{j=1}^{M^2}\omega_{ij}^2 y_j^2\right) \tag{2}$$

This algorithm applies well to situations where the target class subspaces are completely separable, with distinct boundaries. However, as mentioned earlier, many subspaces within the N-dimensional money laundering feature space are not separable, as some launderers behave very similar to or exactly the same as genuine account holders. Consequently, the neural network algorithm must possess a probabilistic component.

The PRCE algorithm replaces the unit step activation function of the second layer with an exponential one. This renders the following activation function:

$$y_i^2 = e^{\left(-u_i^2\right)}, u_i^2 = \left|y - \underline{\omega_i^1}\right|^2 \tag{3}$$

For the output layer, the activation function is:

$$y_i^3 = \sum_{j=1}^{M^2}\omega_{ij}^2 y_j^2 \tag{4}$$

The PRCE algorithm is trained in two stages. The first stage consists of the deposition of the prototypes (neurons) according to the values of each input vector.

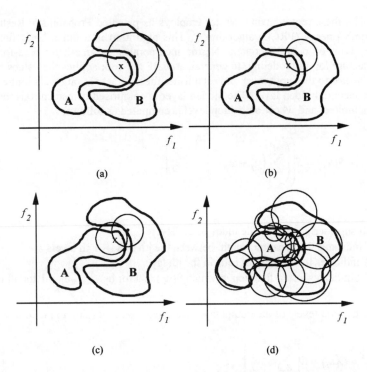

(a)　　　　　　　　　　　(b)

(c)　　　　　　　　　　　(d)

Figure 2: (a) Following the deposition of one prototype in region B, represented by the "•", a training vector representing class A is deposited within the activation region of this second layer cell. (b) That second layer prototype is reduced until vector X falls outside of that prototype. (c) Further prototypes are added to the second layer, reducing when a vector of the opposite class falls within their region of influence. (d) Each of the two subspaces is tiled out with probabilistic prototypes of varying sizes.

In the first training stage of the PRCE algorithm, prototypes (neurons) are deposited in the N-dimensional feature space according to the values of each training feature vector. When, as in Figure2-b, a vector of an opposite class falls within the influence region of an existing prototype, a prototype's size is reduced until it no longer contains the vector of the opposing class. Further prototypes are deposited (Figure 2-c), with their sizes reduced as vectors of the opposing class fall within their region of influence. Finally (Figure 2-d), the various feature subspaces are tiled with the prototypes of varying sizes.

In the case of a money-laundering neural network model, as with other risk management problems, prototypes contain vectors of both classes, necessitating the probabilistic component of the algorithm. In the second training stage, probability density functions are generated according to the frequency with which patterns of each class fall into each prototype[7]. Therefore, counters of vectors of each class falling into each prototype are maintained, and are associated with the weights of the second layer ω^2_{ij}. These weights are then incremented during training when a correctly identified vector causes firing in a middle-layer neuron according to the following:

$$\omega^2_{ij}(t+1) = \omega^2_{ij}(t) + 1 \qquad (5)$$

These weights are not incremented when vectors are not correctly identified.

In model development, we find that prototype shrinkage has little effect on the performance of the model. Further, it is necessary to generate larger numbers of smaller prototypes to optimally separate between the good and laundered transactions. This is due to a large number of good and laundered accounts having similar, although separable, behaviors. That is, it is necessary to tile out the feature subspaces of interest with small prototypes to allow the model to separate between the target classes.

5   Data considerations

While the neural network algorithm is an important component of risk management modeling, the data used to develop and test the model is equally critical. The data can well be considered the life-blood of the model, without which even the best pattern recognition engine is unable to produce a useful model. The following data and model performance information is hypothesized, but we believe that the proportional integrity of the data is such as to allow for inferences and generalizations.

The first data consideration is whether to use a collection of data from a number of institutions to develop a model, or to develop a model on data from that one institution only. In developing risk management models for institutions around the world, Nestor has found that models developed uniquely on that institution's data outperform models developed on a conglomerate of data.

The next consideration in assembling data for model development is to identify which transactions, of which type and from which accounts to collect, preprocess, generate features on and present to the neural network. While this issue is not as readily resolved, as with all other modeling strategy questions, Nestor determines this empirically. We initially collect and retain in the training data set all transaction types from all account types. Next, through feature analysis and a number of modeling strategies, we ferret out those transaction and account types that, when left in the training data, detract from model performance. As money-laundering patterns are somewhat unique to each institution, the definition of those transactions and accounts that must be removed from the data is typically determined during the modeling project.

Once the model development and testing data set is defined, it is necessary to sample the data, then validate that the sample represents the unsampled, natural population of data. To accomplish this – and ensure that performance gains obtained on the sampled data would be proportionately represented on the natural data – Nestor applies a range of non-parametric tests across the sampled and natural data.

After the complete, unsampled data is gathered, the data is assembled on the minority, target, class and the money laundered transactions. This is perhaps the greatest challenge of the modeling project. For example, an institution's risk manager may feel that as many as 2% of the transactions were laundered, but they could identify only 1% of those laundered transactions. Therefore, approximately 99% of the laundered transactions are mislabeled as good. Since there is no way to identify these, the model is presented with many of these in the training data. This presents an enormous challenge as training the neural network on so many mislabeled laundered transactions can, if not addressed, raise the incidence of false negatives significantly. Further, when testing the model and calculating its performance, transactions that receive high scores and are labeled as good could actually be correct detections, but would be considered false positives due to being mislabeled as good. While the details of how Nestor overcomes this challenge are proprietary, it is important to note that this represents the single greatest challenge of money laundering detection model development. Typical data and model characteristics are summarized in Table 1.

Data is segmented into a training and held-aside testing set to ensure that performance figures are not biased as a result of having tested on the training set. After sampling and labeling the data, a significant number of features are developed for presentation to the neural network. That is, training the model directly on the data fields resident in the original data, without first deriving feature representations from it, would result in an extremely poorly performing model. Hundreds of features are typically developed. An example of such features is the number of deposits in a particular time period.

After model features have been generated, it is necessary to define the optimal subset of features. This optimum model feature set is that set which, when one feature is removed from it or added to it, the model performance will decrease. As the features present non-linear, non-gaussian distributions, it is necessary to apply a number of automated statistical and neural techniques to define the optimum feature set. One example of these techniques is the generation of uni-dimensional feature value versus value frequency plots for each of the two target classes, for each feature. While features which offer separation in these plots will add performance to the model, features which do not offer separation on one dimension must be included in further model steps, as some features only offer separation when combined with others.

Model type	Custom
Total number of accounts in unsampled data set	500,000
Total number of transactions in unsampled data set	10,000,000
Number of transactions in model data set	1,000,000
Number of transactions in training data set	833,333
Number of transactions in testing data set	166,666
Number of laundered transactions in unsampled data	20,000
Number of identified laundered accounts	20
Number of laundered transactions in modeling data	200

Table 1: Modeling and testing data characteristics

6   Model performance

The performance figures presented in this article represent typical performance of the neural network system. Actual performance data from a case study have been altered to fully preserve the confidentiality of the institution. However, the findings have been proportionality maintained to allow us to present conclusions.

Following feature generation, optimum feature subset definition and model development with the PRCE algorithm, Nestor generates a number of models, applying a variety of modeling strategies that increase performance.

Figure 3 displays the performance of a model in terms of the percent of money-laundered accounts detected versus account false positive ratio. Implicit in the curve is model score, where a higher score indicates a higher probability of the account being used to launder money. The highest scores are at the left-most portion of the curve, with the scores decreasing as the account false positive ratio increases. Reading from the curve, the model detects slightly over 30% of the laundered accounts at an account false positive ratio of 50:1.

These performance figures should be tempered with the fact that the denominator of the percent account detection rate is 20. This represents the total number of accounts identified prior to project commencement. It is possible that a number of the accounts that received high scores (were considered to be laundered accounts by the model), and were subsequently labeled as good, were actually laundered. Similarly, it is possible that laundered accounts re-labeled as good could fall below the highest score implicit in the above curve, worsening performance. Therefore, the final performance of the model can only accurately be determined once it is in production.

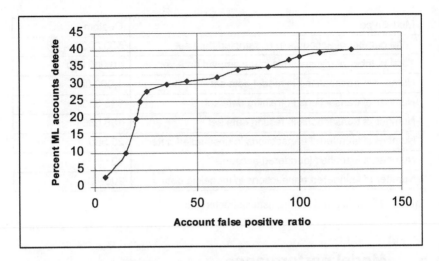

Figure 3: Performance of a neural network money laundering detection model

In spite of the poor labels, it is possible nonetheless to compare model performance with the detection rates provided by an institution's legacy rules-based system. According to available figures, an institution typically detects approximately 10 laundered accounts per year under a rules-based system, at 40:1 account false-positive ratio. The neural network model, by comparison, detects 30% of the 20 accounts in only one month of testing data, at a better account false-positive ratio. Therefore, the model will detect approximately 7 times as many accounts as the rules-based system in the same time period, and this figure could increase were all laundered accounts in the data identified.

7   Software and hardware requirements

Nestor develops neural network models on the NT and Unix platforms, with the majority of software being in-house utilities that have been specifically developed for risk-management model generation. Additionally, Nestor employs industry-standard sorting, database and statistical packages as well as custom utilities. A significant amount of disk and processor resources are required, as most large institutions requiring the models have large amounts of data for preprocessing and sampling.

It is important to note that, while a high-quality neural network model is an integral component of any successful money laundering detection system, the final system must offer a total solution, not simply a software package. For example, the final solution might consist of the model, a production-ready scoring engine to score the transactions, and an integrated case management system with an intuitive graphical user interface to allow the institution to review alerts, generate and alter rules and apply appropriate workflow and queuing strategies. Finally, the solution must include comprehensive user training and support for the life of the installation.

The scoring engine is that software component that scores transactions as they are presented to the core processing machine in production. Figure 4 depicts the neural network-scoring engine as it is presented with transaction and historical data and outputs scored transactions. The scoring engine applies to each record a score that represents the probability that the transaction is laundered. The higher the score is, the higher the probability of money laundering.

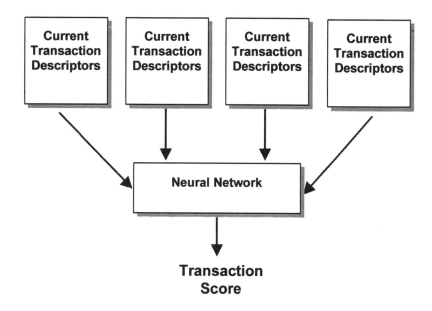

Figure 4: Use of neural network model in production scoring engine

Figure 5 presents the complete money laundering detection solution, Nestor's PRISM Money Laundering Detection solution. The PRISM scoring engine resides on the production machine, normally a mainframe or Tandem processor. This production machine typically resides on a local area network (LAN), on which the PRISM GUI resides. The GUI is a client-server application that is comprised of a thin client, the reviewer workstations, and the server process, which allows for extensive workflow management, rule generation and alteration and report generation.

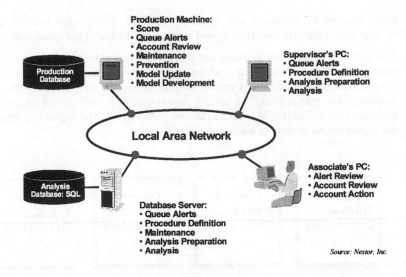

Figure 5: Complete PRISM production installation including scoring engine and GUI

The PRISM GUI server requires an NT processor with sufficient disk and processor resources to accommodate the size of the institution's portfolio of accounts. Similarly, the production machine should have sufficient free CPU and DASD resources to allow for scoring of all transaction data. PRISM is capable of scoring at rates of over 100 transactions per second when sufficient resources are available.

Transactions are sent to the PRISM scoring engine for scoring. The scoring engine may filter out particular accounts which are known to be genuine, and which cannot be compromised by a launderer. Once scored by the model, the transactions are sent to the server via a local area network (LAN). The server places the transaction in an appropriate queue. As the GUI allows for the generation of a variety of rules, some of which may be needed to satisfy governmental laundering review laws, and some of which may be for suspicious transaction detection, all transactions are sent to the system's GUI, regardless of the score, so that they can be processed by the rules-based engine.

8 Model update

As mentioned earlier, a high-quality pattern-recognition algorithm will possess functionality that allows institutions to incorporate recent laundering trends into the model without the need to send data to the detection system for a complete model rebuild. By using more recent transaction data, the system is more adept at detecting new and emerging money laundering schemes. Nestor's PRCE algorithm offers this level of functionality.

Model update is essentially comprised of the second training phase of the algorithm that phase in which the local probabilities of each neuron are computed. This mode of operation can be performed by the user in production, with little knowledge of the model development process. A minimum of two months of data must be extracted, labeled and sampled. Features in the model must be generated and the model must be updated on the resulting data. The test data is then scored with the existing and the updated model, and performance of the models is compared. If the performance of the updated model exceeds that of the existing model, the updated model is released into production. Otherwise, the existing model remains in production. Nestor suggests that users update the model once every three months, although some users have executed it more frequently.

Model update is appropriate for the normal behavior changes launderers, and genuine account holders, exhibit, and for the growth, or contraction, portfolios normally experience. It is not a substitute for acquisitions of completely new portfolios, extensive seasonal volume changes, or for a complete model rebuild once each 18 – 24 months.

9 Conclusion

Financial institutions and regulatory sectors of governments are becoming increasing aware of the alarmingly high incidence of money laundering – and of the destructive force it can have when perpetrated against a financial entity and an economy. Custom money laundering detection neural network models can be developed using transaction data in cases where noisy or very limited target class data is available. These models have been proven to detect significantly more money laundered accounts than traditional rules-based systems, and at better false-positive ratios. Once integrated into a complete risk management solution, the neural network model can complement the overall system, assist financial institutions in meeting the mandatory suspicious transaction reporting requirements, and provide a solid safeguard for an institution's reputation for integrity.

References

1. J. Madinger and S. Zalopany. 1999. In *Money Laundering: A guide for criminal investigators.* (CRC Press)

2. Financial Action Task Force on Money Laundering. Feb. 2000. *Report on Money Laundering Typologies – 1999 – 2000.*

3. C. Intriago, Publisher. *Money Laundering Alert.*

4. D.L. Reilly, L.N. Cooper and C. Elbaum. 1982. A neural model for category learning. *Biol. Cybern*, **45**, 35-41.

5. D.L. Reilly, C.L. Scofield, C. Elbaum and L.N. Cooper. 1987. Learning system architectures composed of multiple learning modules. In *Proc. IEEE First Int. Conf. on Neural Networks*, San Diego, CA, vol. II, 495-503.

6. S. Ghosh and D.L. Reilly. Credit card fraud detection with a neural network. *Forthcoming.*

7. C.L. Scofield, D.L. Reilly, C. Elbaum and L.N. Cooper. 1988. Pattern class degeneracy in an unrestricted storage density memory. In *Neural Information Processing Systems* (D.Z. Anderson, ed.), Denver, CO. (American Institute of Physics, New York, NY), 674-682.

Chapter 11

Utilising Fuzzy Logic and Neurofuzzy for Business Advantage

Bill Edisbury, Roger England and Stewart Hanson
Npower Ltd.

1   An introduction to Fuzzy Logic

How can a logic, which is "fuzzy", be useful? Professor Lotfi Zadeh, the inventor of fuzzy logic, contends that a computer cannot solve problems as well as human experts unless it is able to think in the characteristic manner of a human being.

As humans, we often rely on imprecise expressions like "usually", "expensive", or "far", but the comprehension of a computer is limited to a black-white, everything-or-nothing, true-false mode of thinking. In this context, Lotfi Zadeh emphasises the fact that we easily let ourselves be dragged along by a desire to attain the highest possible precision without paying attention to the imprecise character of reality.

There are many subjects who do not fit into the precise categories of the conventional set theory: The set of "all triangles" or "all the guys named John" is easy to handle with conventional theory. Either somebody's name is John or it is not, there is no other status in between. The set of "all intelligent researchers" or "all the people with an expensive car", however, is much more complicated and cannot be handled easily by a "digital" mode of thinking.

Within conventional logic, terms can be only "true" or "false". Fuzzy logic allows a generalisation of conventional logic, it provides for terms like "almost true" or "partially false". Because of this, fuzzy logic cannot be directly processed on computers, sets of rules to use these terms have to be input and a special program called an "Inference Engine" must transform them into computer instructions. Fuzzy logic software packages are available, from which similar results can be obtained, but since, in the experience of the authors, one package, *fuzzy*TECH from Inform GmbH, is superior. This chapter relates to the use of it.

1.1   Fuzzy Logic using the FuzzyTECH software package

FuzzyTECH provides an Inference Engine, and a complete, graphical development environment by which an entire fuzzy logic system can be developed without writing a single line of code. With such a toolset it is possible to "draw" the system structure, all the variables and the rule sets just as you would draw with any other graphic program, and your fuzzy logic system with all its components is automatically created for you. The creation process is so fast that tests and optimisation procedures typically take more time and effort than the actual design of the fuzzy logic system. *fuzzy*TECH provides a complete set of visual tools, including eight different debug modes, for an optimum testing and simulation environment and also four graphical analyser functions to support the verification of the rule sets through the data.

*fuzzy*TECH can be used as a stand-alone application by using the interfaces provided, or in an integrated form in other software tools, notably Access and Excel. Within the fuzzy logic package there is a "Fuzzy Design Wizard" which guides the developer step by step through defining the input and output linguistic variables, and their fuzzifying membership functions, and the rules to be used in the inference. This allows a beginner to set up a fuzzy logic system without spending a long introductory time with the software, and an experienced developer can design the prototype of a complex system in just a few minutes.

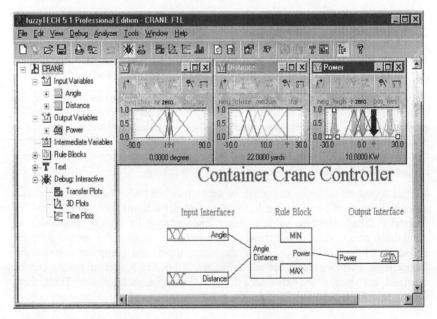

Figure 1: Fuzzy logic design

1.2   The NeuroFuzzy module

There are many applications where it is easier to define the desired system behaviour, or part of it, through examples rather than through manual creation of the rules or the linguistic variables. This is the realm of the NeuroFuzzy module within *fuzzy*TECH, automatically generating and optimising not only the fuzzy logic rules and their weights from the available data, but also optimising the membership functions.

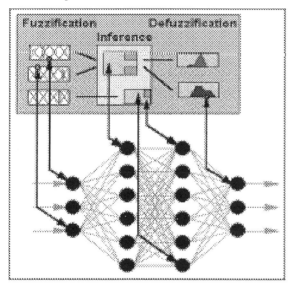

Figure 2: Neuro fuzzy architecture

The NeuroFuzzy Module integrates neural network technologies in order to train fuzzy logic systems. In contrast to conventional neural network solutions, the entire training process and the resulting fuzzy logic system remains completely explanatory due to the white-box nature of fuzzy logic.

The employed training technology is based on an extended fuzzy logic inference method called Fuzzy Associative Memories (FAM). A FAM is a fuzzy logic rule with an associated weight. Such FAM rules can be viewed as generalised neurons in a neural net, see figure 2, whose plausibility is calculated through modified error back propagation.

The NeuroFuzzy Module can also be used to optimise existing fuzzy logic systems. Starting with an existing system, it interactively tunes rule weights and membership function definitions so that the system converges to the behaviour represented by the data sets. Specific rules and membership functions can be locked, if required for safety for example. The entire learning process is visualised, and any fuzzy logic system generated by the NeuroFuzzy module can be further optimised and verified manually.

1.3   Extended fuzzy technologies

In addition to the common methods of fuzzy logic, there are various expanded fuzzy technologies in *fuzzy*TECH. *FuzzyTECH* provides seven different defuzzification methods and eight types of membership functions, including the S-shape functions, which are often used in business applications. Other functionality available includes:

- Support of normalised rule sets. Complex applications can easily cause confusing rules, using different operators, chaos of parentheses, and complicated "if-then-else" statements. Such constructs can destroy the advantages of fuzzy logic systems, like clarity and easy expansion, so a different approach is used, by providing normalised rule sets and graphical structure editors. Applying normalised rule sets has the additional advantage that the rules can be transformed automatically and developed easily in matrix form, which is often more readable than text or table form in the case of huge and complex systems. FuzzyTECH provides all three-presentation forms (text, table, and matrix), while also allowing for switching between them or using them in mixed formats.

- Inference methods. Aside from the standard fuzzy inference methods (MAX-MIN, MAX-PROD), fuzzyTECH also supports the BSUM operator (Bounded-Sum). This operator considers the so-called "support rules" which support the current firing rule.

- Fuzzy operators: fuzzyTECH provides families of generalised operators for fuzzy inference, from which you can create a desired operator through free parameterisation. There are three operator families available: Min-Max, Avg-Max, and Gamma. The Min-Max family represents the "traditional" AND OR fuzzy operators. The Gamma family is most suited to represent the human characteristics of compensated decision behaviour, but is computationally expensive. The Avg-Max family is a less accurate version of the Gamma operator family, optimised with regards to computing efficiency.

2   Fuzzy Logic in business and finance

2.1   Fuzzy-enhanced score card for leasing risk assessment

To automate the risk assessment evaluation for car leasing contracts, BMW Bank GmbH of Germany and Inform Software GmbH of Germany have developed a fuzzy-enhanced score card system. The primary goal of BMW Bank was to take the decision process away from the bank and give it to the car dealer. This allows the dealer to obtain approval whilst dealing with the customer, rather than waiting for BMW Bank to approve a leasing contract.

Decision-support systems streamline workflow

The fuzzy-enhanced score card system has been integrated with the PC-based software that the dealers use to fill out the contract. These PCs are connected to the German credit history database (SCHUFA) to obtain background data on the applicants. The implemented system involves three different types of fuzzy logic modules that are each applied to different customer types: private, self-employed, and corporate. For private customers, a score card had previously been developed that covered various factors in the decision process such as age, marital status, length of time at present address, or later insolvencies. Because this score card already existed and BMW Bank considered it to perform well; it was used as part of the fuzzy logic decision model for private customers.

Private customers

As it is shown in figure 3, the input variable "ScoreCard" is the result of the score card evaluation. The score card result is used with the other input variables "Unemploy" and "Demographic" in the left rule block to compute a risk profile of the customer himself ("CustProfile"). The input variable "Unemploy" comes from a database that stores the current unemployment rate for the customer's profession. The input variable "Demographic" comes from a database and rates the relative liquidity risk for the customer's place of residence.

The result of this evaluation, "CustProfile," is one input of the right rule block that computes the risk rating for the current leasing contract. In addition to CustProfile, the rule block uses the input variables "Backpaying," "CredHist," and "Ratio." The variable, Backpaying describes how timely the customer has been in paying previous leasing contracts, if a past leasing contract with BMW Bank exists. The variable CredHist stems from the German credit history database (SCHUFA) and describes the customer's history of all his past banking history. The variable Ratio is computed as the amount of the monthly payment divided by the monthly disposable income of the customer.

Corporate customers

Figure 4 shows the structure of the fuzzy logic risk assessment for corporate customers. Here, the decision process is more complicated and involves more input variables.

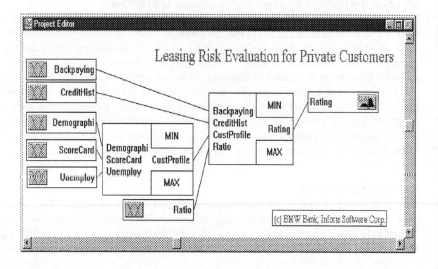

Figure 3: Structure of the fuzzy logic risk assessment for private customers.

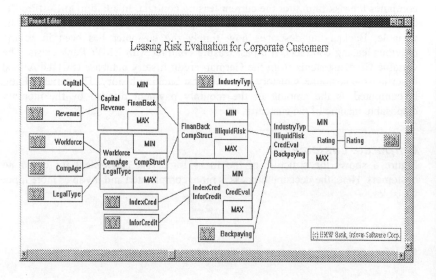

Figure 4: Structure of the fuzzy logic risk assessment for corporate customers.

The rightmost rule block delivers the output variable "Rating" based on the four input variables "IndustryType," "IlliquidRisk," "CredEval," and "Backpaying." IndustryType is an input variable that comes from a database table that maps the type of business to a subjective rating of BMW Bank describing how risky in general a certain type of industry is considered. The variable Backpaying is defined in the same way as for private customers.

The other two input variables of the rightmost rule block stem from other rule blocks. CredEval is a combination of the input variables "IndexCred" and "InforCred." Both come from information service providers that maintain credit ratings for every company in Germany. IlliquidRisk is the fuzzy logic system's evaluation of the risk of this company becoming illiquid. A rule block computes this variable from the financial background evaluation ("FinanBack") and the company structure evaluation ("CompStruct"). The financial background evaluation considers the company's capital basis ("Capital") and its annual revenue ("Revenue"). The company structure evaluation considers the number of employees ("Workforce"), the age of the company ("Age"), and the legal status ("LegalType") of the company.

Implementation at BMW Bank

The total fuzzy logic system involves 413 fuzzy logic rules in three modules. The entire design, test, and verification of the three modules took two person-years effort, and integrating the DLL modules generated by *fuzzy*TECH into the PC-based software for leasing contract management required another person-month. The system is currently in operation at German BMW dealers, and BMW Bank management considers its performance to be equivalent to an experienced leasing contract expert. Although a detailed cost savings analysis is not published by BMW Bank, a quick estimation on the basis of 50,000 leasing contracts per year and a total evaluation time of 30 minutes for each leasing contract (including obtaining credit history information) results in 25,000 person hours, or 14 person years. Compared to the cost of the fuzzy logic decision support system's implementation and maintenance, this saving is quite substantial.

2.2   Software engineering with fuzzy logic

The BMW bank example shows the way that financial services companies obtain and integrate data from different sources. Standards and software engineering are essential to commercial success. The concepts encapsulated by the *fuzzy*TECH software have been incorporated into a further product, Riskshield, a description of which is given here to illustrate the commercial engineering demanded of such packages.

Riskshield (RS) aids fraud detection, by combining traditional statistics, data mining, and pattern recognition with fuzzy logic rule-based decision methods and neural network techniques to provide autoadaptability. All RS software products are based on client/server type architecture using advanced software development methods (Windows/NT, C++, DCOM, and ODBC). They consist of the three components: Decision Engine, Investigation Workflow, and Supervisory Workflow

- The RS Decision Engine is a server component that analyses each transaction and evaluates its likelihood of being fraudulent. For each suspicious transaction, the Decision Engine generates a "case". A case combines the transaction information with all relating information to the potential fraud case.
- Each case is put into queues that are processed by the RS Investigation Workflow. The Investigation Workflow is a client component that supports all steps for an auditor to investigate and close a case. The Investigation Workflow is highly adaptable to various environments and business processes.
- RS's Supervisory Workflow is a complete development environment for the analysis of abuse patterns and the definition of effective countermeasures. The Supervisory Workflow combines intelligent software techniques in an MS-Office like software environment that lets the abuse analysts configure the RS Decision Engine. Advanced statistical features deliver sophisticated performance analyses of RS's operation.

In addition, the Supervisory Workflow contains a documentation component that automatically generates ISO 9001 compliant documentation of a decision strategy. The Decision Engine can run on MVS mainframe type computer systems, integrated as a COBOL library, both for IMS and CICS environments, as well as on UNIX, integrated as an ANSI-C library, or Windows/NT type server computer systems, where it is integrated as an ActiveX component. Both Supervisory and Investigation Workflow software run on Windows/NT clients, and to connect the Workflow component to the Decision Engine, any type of network can be used.

3   Fuzzy logic in process engineering

In recent years, fuzzy logic has demonstrated its potential in Engineering applications and industrial automation applications, often running in conjunction with programmable logic controllers (PLCs). While PLCs work well when the process under control is in a stable condition, they do not cope well with:

- The presence of strong disturbances (non-linearity)
- Time-varying parameters of the process (non-linearity)
- Presence of dead times

The reason for this is that a PLC controller assumes the process to behave in a strictly linear fashion. While this simplification can be made in a stable condition, strong disturbances can push the process operation point far away from the operating set point. Once this happens, the linear assumption usually does not work any more. The same happens if a process changes its parameters over time. In these cases, the extension or replacement of PLCs with fuzzy controllers has been shown to be more feasible than using conventional state controllers or adaptive approaches.

3.1 Multi-variable control

The real potential of fuzzy logic in industrial automation lies in the straightforward way fuzzy logic renders possible the design of multi-variable controllers.

In many applications, keeping a single process variable constant can be done well using a PID or bang-bang type controller. However, set-point values for all these individual control loops are often still set manually by operators. The operators analyse the process condition, and tune the values to optimise the operation. Fuzzy logic enables the capture of that operator expert knowledge.

PID and bang-bang type controllers can also only cope with one variable. This usually results in several independently operating control loops, which are not able to "talk to each other". In the cases where it is desirable or necessary to exploit interdependencies of physical variables, a complete mathematical model of the process has to be set up as well as the differential equations that are necessary for the implementation of a solution. In the world of industrial automation, this is rarely feasible because:

- Creating a mathematical model for a real-word problem can involve years of work.
- Most mathematical models involve extensive simplifications and linearisations that require "fudge" factors to optimise the resulting controller later on.
- Tuning the fudge factors of a controller derived from a mathematical model is "fishing in the dark", because optimising the system at one operating point using global factors usually degrades the performance at other operating points.

This is where fuzzy logic provides an elegant and highly efficient solution to the problem. Fuzzy logic lets the engineer design supervisory multi-variable controllers from operator experience and experimental results rather than from mathematical models.

A possible structure of a fuzzy logic based control system in industrial automation applications is exemplified by Figure 5. Each single process variable is kept constant by a PID controller, while the set-point values for the PID controller stem from the fuzzy logic system. This arrangement is typical for applications like control of several temperature zones of an oven, fire zone control in waste incineration plants, or dosing control in wastewater treatment plants.

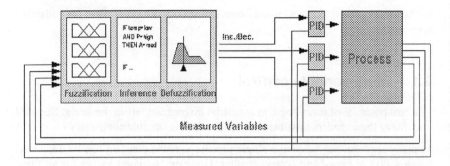

Figure 5: Using a Fuzzy Logic Controller to Determine the Set Values for Underlying PID Control Loops

Merging fuzzy logic and PLCs – The fuzzyPLC

Figure 5 illustrates why it is very desirable to integrate conventional control engineering techniques, such as ladder logic or instruction list language for digital logic and PID control blocks tightly together with fuzzy logic functionality. This is the concept behind the *fuzzy*PLC, which uses a highly integrated two-chip solution.

In the *fuzzy*PLC, an analogue ASIC handles the analogue/digital interfaces at industry standard 12-bit resolution, and "Snap-On" modules can extend the periphery for large applications of up to about 100 signals. An integrated field bus connection, based on RS485, provides further expansion by networking. The conventional and the fuzzy logic computations are handled by a 16/32-bit RISC microcontroller and memory cards using flash technology can expand the internal RAM of 256 KB. The operating system and communication routines were developed by Klockner-Moeller and are based on a commercial real time multitasking kernel. The fuzzy inference engine is implemented and integrated into the operating system so that scan times of less than one millisecond are possible, and it is programmed by an enhanced version of the fuzzy logic development software, *fuzzy*TECH. Thus, the *fuzzy*PLC is capable of solving quite complex and fast industrial automation problems in spite of its compact and low price design.

3.2   Neurofuzzy control in washing machines

Washing machines in Europe are different from those used in the U.S.A and in Japan. The European washing process is much more complicated, taking up to 2 hours, though water consumption is much lower, typically ranging from 50 to 60 litres (13 - 18 gallons). Also, white laundry, such as underwear, tableware, and bed sheets, is washed at temperatures up to 95°C (203°F), hence, washing machines do not use the hot water from the house but rather heat up the water electrically.

The complex washing process consists of multiple wash, process, bleach, rinse and spin steps. To control this, modern washing machines use micro-controller hardware and multiple sensors:

- Tachometer for the drum spin.
- Analogue pressure sensor for the water level (Figure 6).
- Digital sensor to detect strong unevenness during spinning.
- Digital sensor to detect excessive foam.

To determine the optimal washing program, actual laundry load (type and volume) of the washing machine must be known. Sensors, which could measure these parameters directly, are expensive and unreliable. Hence, the objective for AEG was to design a system that estimated the actual laundry load only from the existing sensors.

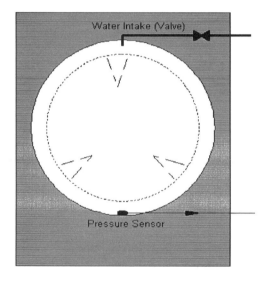

Figure 6: Washing machine sensors

Water absorption curves

Figure 7 plots the pressure sensor curve over time. The plot starts when the water intake valves first opens.

- The water intake valve opens at T_0. At T_1, the water level reached set value. This duration does not depend much on the laundry load since the laundry in the non-rotating drum does not absorb much water.
- At T_1, the drum starts to rotate in a certain rhythm, causing the laundry to absorb water. Since the drum holds the weight of the laundry, the water pressure measured by the sensor decreases. At a later time T_2, the new pressure is stored and the difference to the pressure at T_1 gives an indication of the absorption speed.
- At T_2, the current water pressure is stored again. It gives an indication of the absorption volume, as the laundry is mostly saturated at this time. At T_2, the water valve is opened again to fill up the water level to the set point.

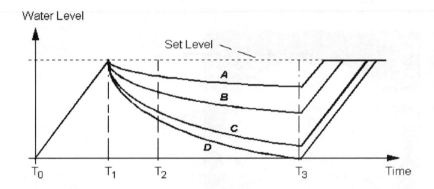

Figure 7: Water Level in the Drum of the Washing Machine during Initial Water Intake. By Interpreting the Curves, an Estimation of Laundry Type and Volume Is Possible.

As there is no mathematical model relating the water absorption curves to the laundry load, AEG decided to use fuzzy logic to design a solution based on the knowledge of their washing experts. Figure 8 shows the structure of the fuzzy logic system that estimates the water requirement in washing and rinse steps. The input variables of the fuzzy logic system stem from the water absorption curve.

The upper fuzzy logic rule block estimates the water requirement during washing (WaterLev1) from absorption speed (AbsorbSp) and absorption volume (AbsorbVol). Both these input variables are calculated from T1 - T0 and T2 - T1. The two lower fuzzy logic rule blocks estimate the water requirement during rinse (WaterLev2). Inputs to the intermediate rule block are water requirement during washing, as determined by the upper rule block, and total absorption volume. These are combined to describe the total absorption characteristic (AbsorbChar). This variable is not an output of the fuzzy logic system, but only used as one input for the lower fuzzy logic rule block.

The lower rule block estimates the water requirement during the rinse step (WaterLev2). Other inputs are the soap ration, the number of rinse steps given by the selected washing program, and the selected speed of the spin step. All membership functions are of Standard type (Z, Lambda, and S) and the defuzzification employs Centre-of-Maximum (CoM) method.

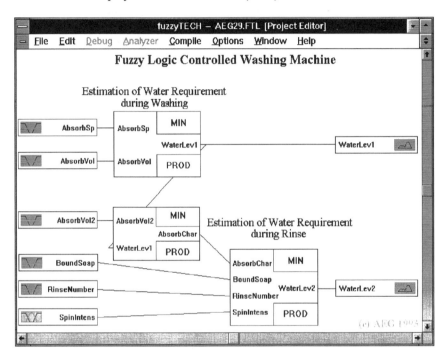

Figure 8: The Multi Level Fuzzy Logic System interprets the water intake function and determines the amount of water to be used in the subsequent washing steps. Also, the further washing program is optimised according to the load.

Fuzzy Logic vs. NeuroFuzzy

The approach of interpreting the water absorption curve to estimate the laundry load is innovative, therefore not much engineering "know-how" on the interpretation of the curves exists. As this "know-how" is essential to manually building a solution with fuzzy logic the first attempt of AEG to find a satisfying set of fuzzy logic rules failed. However, AEG had water absorption curves for various known laundry loads and the washing experts can easily determine the optimal water requirement for these laundry loads. So, using experimental results as training examples, AEG's next try was to use NeuroFuzzy techniques.

Table 1 shows some of these training examples. Here, the left column (Laundry load) lists the materials used for this washing experiment; the next two columns

(Water absorption speed and volume) give parameters from the water absorption curve. The washing experts were shown the first columns with the known load and asked to recommend the optimum water requirement.

The NeuroFuzzy training used the right column as the desired output and the middle two columns as the respective inputs. (The training cannot use the left column since the actual load is not known to the washing machine during operation.) The aim was that the trained fuzzy logic system would respond with the appropriate water level recommendation determined by the measured values of the input variables.

Laundry load	Water absorption speed	Water absorption volume	Water requirement in subsequent washing steps (from expert)
4 kg Wool / 1 kg Cotton	0.67	2.44	3.5
3 kg Wool / 1 kg Cotton	0.61	2.10	3.1
2 kg Wool / 2kg Cotton	0.62	1.99	2.8

Table 1: The sample data for the NeuroFuzzy training has been gained through extensive washing experiments. In each experiment, different laundry types and volumes were used. For each experiment, the washing expert gave his recommendation for the amount of water to be used in subsequent washing steps.

The NeuroFuzzy learning process created 159 rules in the fuzzy logic system shown in Figure 7, small enough to be implemented on the standard 8 bit micro-controller, and the solution was able to estimate the water requirement with a maximum difference from the optimum value of 0.35 litres (0.09 gallons). In an average home, this saves about 20% of the water consumption. As most of the electricity consumed by the washing machine is used to heat up water, 20% of energy is saved too.

4   Medical applications: monitoring glaucoma by means of a neurofuzzy classifier

Glaucoma is a prevalent eye disease. Therefore an early detection of glaucomatous changes within the patient's eye status is very important. This can be done by using 'intelligent monitors' to support the detection process of primary carers. The main function of an intelligent glaucoma monitor is to react as a 'watch dog', 'barking' if critical or suspicious situations are detected, otherwise to lie in a 'sleeping' condition. Both conditions require the assessment and classification of new data sets. The classification has to be done in two different ways, as a differential diagnosis decision and an evaluation of time-dependent changes. This section of the paper describes the classification methods leading to a differential diagnosis decision.

4.1   Input data

The decision of medical experts about glaucomatous changes of a patient's eye rely on the following data sets:

- direct measurable data
- parameter estimations
- unstructured verbal descriptions

Directly measurable data are the intraocular pressure (IOP) given as a real number in a pressure unit (or as a data set of several IOP values as a daily profile) and perimetry data sets. The latter data describe the status of the visual field of the patient measured by special devices (perimeters), which detect the loss in light sensitivity at different stimulus points of the retina (number and locations depend on the applied perimeter type and measuring regime). These locations are stimulated by flashing light of different intensities at different locations within a hemisphere with a background illumination whilst the patient is looking at the centre. The 'answer' as to whether or not a stimulus could be seen is given pressing a response button by the patient. Perimetry is a more subjective measurement than IOP.

During the eye examination estimates are made of several parameters like the cup-disc-ratio (CDR), the location of the excavation or a comparison of the CDR's of the right and left eyes. The CDR and the right-left-difference are given as real numbers (estimated) the location is given in linguistic terms like 'central, inferior, superior'. The CDRs and the differences are transformed by the medical experts into a meta-level of classification, evaluating them as 'normal, increased' etc.

The third information source is the patient's own reports which are mainly given verbally but contain valuable information about the condition at the time point of visiting the ophthalmologist and about changes in this condition.

Based on these data the ophthalmologist has to decide whether or not these data and the related findings belong to glaucomatous findings or not, and additionally what type of action is required. Actions here can be the decision about a shorter or longer interval to the next examination, a medication or a decision about a type of eye surgery (depending on the glaucoma type.).

The goal is to model this decision process, giving decision support to the ophthalmologist. The final decision-maker remains the physician.

4.2   Neural Networks

Due to the fact that it is very difficult to give an exact formal description about how to classify perimetry data, artificial neural networks (ANNs) are used to learn the classification task on the basis of pre-classified perimetry samples. An advantage of the hierarchical classification scheme is the refinement of the input space to 'parts of interest', the glaucomatous perimetries.

The design of the ANN classifier is based on the classification tree shown in Figure 9 (left side). The motivation in modelling the classification tree is to introduce several decision stages, ranging from rather crude decisions like the 'normal'/'pathological' classification up to refined decisions, like the 'questionable'/'probably glaucomatous' classification. The approach in modelling the ANN-perimeter-classifier is to design a specialised ANN for every decision level from the root to the leaves of the classification tree respectively (see Figure 9 right).

Every ANN is trained exclusively on that part of the feature space defined by the set of perimetry samples according to their classification task. This reduces the input dimensionality of every ANN. ANN 1 through ANN 6 classify perimetry data samples respectively. Their output values are interpreted top down according to the classification tree. If for example the ANN 2 classifier gives the result that the perimetry is more 'normal' than 'pathological', more attention to the results of the ANN 3 classifier are given than to the results of the ANN 4, ANN 5 or ANN 6 classifiers. This kind of interpretation is possible due to the fact that RBF networks are used, which do an interpolation between samples of a feature space region.

ANN 1 through ANN 6 were trained by 2/3 and tested/evaluated by 1/3 of the perimetry-sample sets according to the classification tree. Table 2 gives an overview of the sensitivity/specificity evaluation results of the ANN classifiers.

Hierarchy	Sensitivity / Specificity
ANN 1	83 % / 81 %
ANN 2	85 % / 93 %
ANN 3	91 % / 92 %
ANN 4	72 % / 71 %
ANN 5	79 % / 56 %
ANN 6	62 % / 74 %

Table 2: Results of the specialised ANN

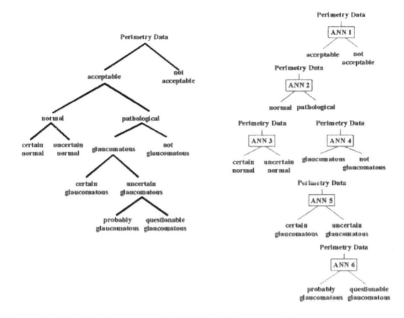

Figure 9: *Classification tree and ANN classifier approach*

4.3   Fuzzy rule sets

The overall decision about the differential diagnosis is given by a fuzzy rule set. The main structure is shown in Figure 10. CDR, IOP and the left-right-difference values are input directly as real numbers, which will be fuzzified by membership functions (MBFs), defined by the medical expert in co-operation with the knowledge engineer. The first rule level combines these values using min-max decision rules to get output values of the first level: These are intraocular hypertension, normotensive glaucoma and all other glaucoma types (glaucoma). The result is given as a membership value to the variable terms 'yes' and 'no'. These provisional results are used as an output and input to the next rule level, respectively. The second rule level gets additional input from the classification of perimetry data.

The classification of the perimetry data is input at all three hierarchical levels. Starting with the highest one (normal-pathological-not acceptable) down to the deeper classification of normal and pathological/glaucomatous classes. These methods can be incorporated in the *fuzzy*TECH software package. The final decision outcome (final_glaucoma_yes etc.) is combined to 'situation classes' like 'glaucomatous changes', 'suspect glaucomatous changes', 'pathological but seemingly not glaucomatous changes', 'normal'. This final decision is presented to the user as a verbal message with a short description and the possibility to get further information by sending a query to the ophthalmic knowledge-based information system.

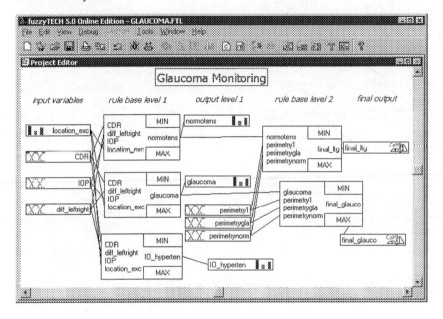

Figure 10: Main structure and fuzzy rule set

5   Prediction of aircraft performance after take-off

The UK National Air Traffic Control proposed a demonstrator that involved using neural networks and fuzzy logic data mining techniques to determine whether long term historic knowledge of aircraft performance could improve vertical track prediction for departing aircraft. Current tools, including collision avoidance systems, predict the future height of an aircraft by extrapolating from its current height and assuming it will continue to climb at its current rate, estimated from the aircraft's recent track history.

Two minutes of radar track data for every aircraft departing from Heathrow was available, which as well as providing 3 dimensional position fixes every 4 seconds for 2 minutes, gave track velocities for the first radar cycle, and an aircraft type, operator, departure routing and intended flight destination was associated with each track. All of this information is currently available to NATS from different data sources.

Npower developed a model that predicted the vertical position of the aircraft 88 seconds ahead, predicting this far rather than at 120 seconds, meant that there were

9 data samples for each aircraft track, given a total data sample of 27000 records. Some of the input data proved to be unsuitable for processing in its presented form, so user knowledge was used to change these inputs into a more suitable format, e.g. the aircraft type data consisted of qualitative inputs like 737, A300, 747 etc, but, given that each aircraft belongs to 1 of 4 speed groupings, has 1 to 4 engines and belongs to 1 of 5 wake-vortex categories, it was decided to replace aircraft type by these three inputs. Similarly operator was grouped by giving the two main operators their own identity number and grouping all the remaining operators into an 'other' group, and aircraft destinations, initially provided as a 4 digit ICAO code, were replaced with distance data.

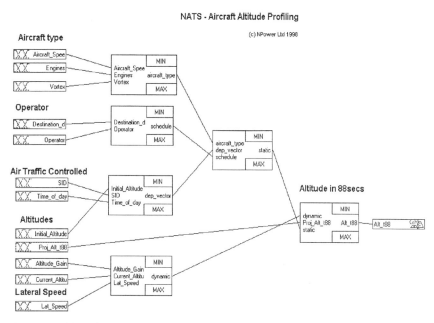

Figure 11: Air traffic control prediction model

The fuzzy logic model had the structure shown in the figure 11. With 12 fuzzy inputs, in order to maintain the understandability of the rules in the system, interim rule blocks (like the nodes in Neural Networks) were introduced into the model structure. The inputs combined in each of the interim rule blocks were related, this is one way in which user knowledge is built into the model.

The NeuroFuzzy component within the *fuzzy*TECH toolset was used to derive the degrees of support for each rule in the various rule blocks, from a training set of around 1000 records.

The developed model was then tested using all 27000 records, comparing the model's predictions for an aircraft's vertical position in 88 seconds against the actual aircraft position in 88 seconds. Figure 12 shows the frequency with which different errors were observed. The errors that would have been observed by predicting an aircraft's vertical position using linear extrapolation are also plotted on this graph for comparison. It can be seen that the fuzzy logic predictor tended to have smaller prediction errors than linear extrapolation predictions.

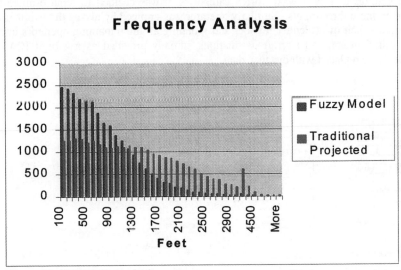

Figure 12: Frequency analysis

Other analysis showed that there is additional information in historical track data statistics, generated from the track data prior to the data from the radar cycle that is used for the current prediction, that could improve performance further. It is clear that fuzzy logic has provided a model with better predictive performance than the linear extrapolation.

NATS have shown interest in using the white-box nature of fuzzy logic to look at the rules with the most support in the developed model to see if they can understand why the model has an improved predictive performance, and what factors are influential in the prediction.

To understand how to interpret a Neruofuzzy generated fuzzy logic model, one must look at the three stages of the model, 'fuzzification of inputs', 'fuzzy inference' and 'de-fuzzification of the output'. These three stages are described below for a simple example, providing a fuzzy model for determining the probability of an aircraft levelling off at a particular flight level. There are two inputs to this model, the aircraft type (a large number of discrete aircraft names, e.g. B747) and the vertical velocity of the aircraft 100 feet before the level.

Creating terms and membership functions (MBF's) for each input does the first stage of 'fuzzify the inputs'. E.g. vertical velocity may have two descriptive terms, high and low, and the shape of the MBF's for these terms determine the degree of support for each term for any vertical velocity. These are usually represented in a graphical form for ease of understanding, see figure 13. For example, an aircraft with a vertical velocity A has a membership value of 0.4 of having a 'high' velocity and 0.7 of having a 'low' velocity.

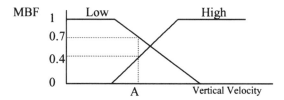

Figure 13: Terms and MBF's for vertical velocity

Although aircraft types are discrete they need to be converted onto a scale in order to place them in membership functions. One way to place aircraft into membership functions could be to sort them in terms of their physical weight. In this model aircraft type is converted into two membership functions, small and large. The two terms for the 'fuzzy output' are levelling and not-levelling.

Fuzzy Inference is performed by creating a rule block linking the 'fuzzy output' to the 'fuzzy inputs', and each rule created in this rule block has a degree of support (DoS) associated with it, that is the confidence that the rule is correct. Example rules may be like those in table 3.

The expert user can enter the rules block, thus capturing expert knowledge, but in this example these rules have be deduced using Neurofuzzy software. *Fuzzy*TECH software generates all the possible rules for a model, then the Neurofuzzy module applies back-propagation techniques to adjust the degree of support associated with each rule in order to minimise the difference between the model's de-fuzzified predictions and required outputs for a set of training data.

Velocity		Type		Fuzzy Output	DOS
Low	&	Small	then	Levelling	1
Low	&	Large	then	Non-Levelling	0.5
High	&	Small	then	Levelling	0.8
High	&	Large	then	Non-Levelling	1

Table 3: Fuzzy rule block

Fuzzy Inference best explained by considering a case of an aircraft. The input variable data for this aircraft produces term membership values of 0.4 for a 'high' velocity and 0.7 for a 'low' velocity, and 1 for it being of 'large' type and 0.5 for 'small' type. Now, considering the first rule in table 3, low velocity is supported by 0.7 and small type by 0.5, AND-ing these in fuzzy logic means take the minimum membership value for these two events, so 0.5. Given that the DoS, confidence, for this rule, is 1 we have 0.5 *1, or 0.5, support for the aircraft levelling.

Working down all the rules using a similar process and totalling complementary outcomes we find that rules 1 and 3 give 0.82 (0.5+0.4*0.8) support for the aircraft levelling, and rules 2 and 4 give 0.75 (0.7*0.5+0.4*1) support for non-levelling.

The last stage of a fuzzy logic system is the 'de-fuzzification', or turning a fuzzy output into a crisp result. One method of de-fuzzification, Centre-of-Maximum, is done by plotting the support for each output term on its respective membership function, and finding the overall centre of gravity. This provides a single value for the probability for aircraft levelling, from our example of 65 percent, see figure 14.

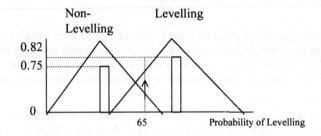

Figure 14: Defuzzification

NATS believe that as well as allowing uncertainty to be modelled, building models using fuzzy logic can provide a number of benefits. It generates rules that can be conventionally programmed, and because it simplifies decision rules it can reduce programming complexity. It can provide an effective means for modelling non-linear relationships and allows both quantitative and qualitative data to be used in modelling. It provides transparent rules that can be validated. It allows for business knowledge to be captured, as the model is generated using the natural language used in a business. The operational use of such techniques will lead to greater safety as the airways get more crowded in the new millenium.

Index